W9-AQE-485

FREEDOM
AND
EQUALITY

FREEDOM AND EQUALITY

Addresses by Harry S. Truman

David Horton, editor

UNIVERSITY OF MISSOURI PRESS

COLUMBIA

PREFACE

This volume contains nine addresses and messages to the Congress, on the subjects of freedom and equality, by the Honorable Harry S. Truman, United States Senator and thirty-second President of the United States.

The first three selections deal with what is currently one of the most difficult problems facing the people and governments of the United States in the realm of human rights: the treatment of our largest minority group, the Negroes.

Five of the remaining six speeches and messages of Mr. Truman are concerned with the problem of meeting the internal threat of Communism without destroying the freedoms guaranteed by the Bill of Rights.

The final document—the veto message on the Immigration and Nationality Act of 1952—deals with both freedom and equality, with both the problem of Communism and the problem of fair treatment of minorities.

To provide the reader with some knowledge of the background and general setting of Mr. Truman's speeches and messages, a brief introductory chapter reviewing Mr. Truman's record on freedom and equality is included.

The pleasant task of preparing this volume for publication was made possible by a grant from the John Findley Green Foundation, under whose auspices President Truman delivered the address, "What Hysteria Does to Us," Chapter VIII of this book, at Westminster College, Fulton, Missouri, on April 12, 1954.

I wish to acknowledge the cooperation and encouragement given to me by President Robert L. D. Davidson of Westminster College and by President Truman himself, with whose permission this work was undertaken. For valuable assistance rendered in typing and proofreading, sincere thanks go to Mrs. Jackie Stapleton and to my wife, Janet.

Fulton, Missouri   D. H.
March 1, 1960

CONTENTS

INTRODUCTION

Freedom and equality are among the most important concepts in the philosophy of the democratic state. Deeply rooted in America's past and in our Anglo-Saxon heritage, they have come to us by way of the long stream of history which has its wellsprings in the ancient worlds of the Romans, the Greeks, and the Jews.

In contemporary times as in past centuries, freedom and equality have been ideals aspired to but never fully attained. Always widely magnetic in their appeal, they have nevertheless been constantly challenged and sometimes defeated by prejudice, by fears arising from economic, social, and political insecurity, and by competing interests of individuals and groups. Throughout history, the champions of freedom and equality have always had to fight to maintain and, if possible, to advance these ideals, against strong opposition.

In our own day, one of the staunchest champions of freedom and equality has been Harry S. Truman who, in almost two decades as Senator and as President, established a remarkably clear and consistent record in his fight for human rights. Mr. Truman's role in this area was in keeping with his own view that the President should provide strong, positive leadership—a view shared by such recent students of the Presidency as Clinton Rossiter, who stated: "The President is the American people's one authentic trumpet, and he has no higher duty than to give a clear and certain sound."[1]

Despite a family background based on southern tradition, Mr. Truman endeavored throughout his political career to improve the status and treatment of the Negro, as well as of other minority groups.

---

[1] Clinton Rossiter, *The American Presidency* (The New American Library edition, 1956), p. 23.

Some of Mr. Truman's critics and political opponents have charged, of course, that his fight on behalf of minorities was motivated by political expediency—by a desire to win the votes of minority groups in political campaigns.[2]

In the election of 1948, when Mr. Truman and the Democratic Party made the strongest and most specific stand in favor of civil rights taken in recent decades, there was ample warning that such action might cost Mr. Truman a significant number of electoral votes in the South, and it did. On the other hand, it was possible that a strong liberal stand on civil rights would win votes in the large cities of such key states as New York and Illinois. From a political viewpoint, it was a very real gamble, or at best a calculated risk, to splinter the Democratic Party on the civil rights issue and to attempt to cut the left-of-center vote away from Henry Wallace and his Progressive Party. Political expediency might have dictated to a more timid candidate that he compromise on the civil rights issue, hold the southern vote solid, and still attempt to appear liberal enough to win the votes of the large northern cities. Mr. Truman, however, was not a timid candidate: he did not compromise, but staked his political career on taking a bold stand on civil rights, risking loss of part of the South, and trying to make up for it by winning more votes elsewhere.

In one of the most stunning upsets in the history of presidential elections, this bold strategy produced victory for Mr. Truman. Taken by itself, of course, this might mean simply that he was more shrewd, but not necessarily less expedient.

To see the situation in perspective, it is necessary to look at least briefly at the historical setting out of which Mr. Truman's line of action on civil rights grew. The problem of fair treatment of the Negro in America in a sense goes all the way back to 1619, when the first slaves were brought to these shores. Jim Crowism, as such, however, is of relatively recent origin. For example, no general segregation of Negroes was practiced in the South even when the southern whites

---

[2]In the 1958 campaign, for example, it was reported in the press that Republican National Chairman Meade Alcorn had issued a statement October 9, 1958, quoting Representative Frank Boykin, Democrat of Alabama, as having told him that at the White House in 1948 President Truman had said to him: "Frank, I don't believe in this civil rights program any more than you do, but we've got to have it to win." To this Mr. Truman replied: "It just isn't true. As a matter of fact about that time I was getting out a booklet on the need for equality in education and it is still in existence. I don't know what lengths the Republicans will go to distort truth." *St. Louis Post-Dispatch*, October 19, 1958, p. 2A, col. 3-4. *See also* Samuel Lubell, *The Future of American Politics* (2nd ed. rev.; New American Library, 1956), p. 8.

resumed control following the era of Reconstruction, although there were special areas of segregation, as in the churches, in the public schools, in the military forces, and in private social gatherings.[3]

General segregation and disfranchisement of the Negroes in fact did not appear in the South until about the 1890's. At that time "the South's adoption of extreme racism was due not so much to a conversion as it was to a relaxation of the opposition."[4] The opposition of the northern liberals to racism relaxed in the press, in the Supreme Court, and elsewhere for various reasons, including the desire for the reconciliation of northern and southern whites and the venture of the United States into international imperialism, with its concomitant subjection of peoples of color in the Philippines and in other recently acquired possessions. The restraint upon rampant racism exercised by the southern conservative leaders in the period of Redemption and Reunion (beginning in 1877) largely disappeared because such leaders were discredited by financial scandals, were repudiated because of the very liberality of their original racial policies, and otherwise lost popularity because of their overemphasis of property rights and their identification with financial, commercial, and industrial interests. Even Negro leaders like Booker T. Washington adopted a policy of patient submissiveness. The southern radicals in the Populist movement became reconciled with the dominant white conservative leaders and ceased to be militant champions of the rights of Negroes.

Not even the Progressive era of the early twentieth century or World War I, which was "fought to make the world safe for democracy" and in which many Negroes wore the uniform, could stem the rising tide of racial discrimination. Indeed, the fires of racial hatred burned more fiercely than ever in the immediate post-World War I period and in the 1920's, with numerous race riots in the North and border areas and with lynchings and Klan terrorism in the South.

Not until the challenge of the Great Depression called forth the New Deal under the dynamic leadership of Franklin D. Roosevelt was there enough reinvigoration of the liberal elements, North and South, Negro and white, to lay the groundwork for the beginning of a new era in race relations, during and after World War II. Many diverse factors, personal and impersonal, played their part in this mighty struggle to keep the United States from continuing its downward course

---

[3]The account given here and in the next few paragraphs is based on an excellent study by C. Van Woodward, *The Strange Career of Jim Crow* (rev. ed.; New York: Oxford University Press, 1957), *passim.*

[4]*Ibid.,* p. 51.

toward an American *apartheid*. Professor C. Vann Woodward, in *The Strange Career of Jim Crow*,[5] cites such moral forces as those promoted by the Negro himself, through the National Association for the Advancement of Colored People, the National Urban League, and the National Negro Congress; the Negro literary and artistic awakening of the 'twenties and 'thirties; the "social gospel" movement of the Protestant churches; the efforts of Roman Catholics along the same lines; the American faith in equality of opportunity and equality of rights professed in the South and North alike; and the rise of liberals in the South, organized in such groups as the Commission on Interracial Cooperation, the Southern Regional Conference, and the Southern Conference for Human Welfare.

Among the impersonal forces which helped move the racial problem from the stagnant backwaters of sectionalism into the swift main stream of national politics was the great migration of Negroes from the South to the North, with the result that between one-third and one-half of the Negroes in the United States began living outside the South. The effects of this migration were felt most strongly in the large cities, where Negro political potential invited the attention of national leaders of both political parties. Because of wartime and postwar prosperity, more and more Negroes entered into the powerful middle class, gaining attendant prestige and acceptability. Since the foremost foe of the United States in World War II was Nazi Germany (with its abhorrent doctrine of racism), the realization that all racial discrimination is evil was indelibly impressed upon the conscience of America. Russian Communist propaganda in the Cold War held up, for the uncommitted people of color in Asia and Africa to see, every embarrassing discrepancy between the ideal of equality and the reality of discrimination in America, and this pricked the American conscience. Even the dull and the reluctant began to perceive, however dimly or distastefully, that American ideals and self-interest had taken on a new and positive alignment in this area of race relations.

Out of this background and within this context, Harry S. Truman assumed his role in the struggle to achieve better treatment for the Negroes and other minorities in America.

In his early years as United States Senator from Missouri, Mr. Truman did not say much about civil rights on the floor of the Senate, but his actions spoke eloquently enough. Without exception, whenever

[5]See footnote 3.

the opportunity presented itself, Senator Truman acted to provide greater protection for minorities and to afford equal treatment under the law.

For example, Mr. Truman consistently supported anti-lynching bills. In July, 1937, he voted against a motion to table an anti-lynching bill.[6] While presiding temporarily over the Senate in November, 1937, he prevented a southern Senator from engaging in the dilatory tactic of suggesting the absence of a quorum shortly after the roll-call had been taken and while civil rights legislation was pending. His ruling from the chair on this point, when challenged by the Senator against whom it was made, was sustained by a majority of the Senate.[7]

Twice in the Seventy-fifth Congress, third session, in 1938, Senator Truman did what many Senators never do, and signed petitions under the cloture rule (Senate Rule XXII) bringing before the Senate a motion to close debate and thereby to end a filibuster being waged against the anti-lynching bill by southern Senators.[8]

When, in 1940, discrimination was disclosed against members of minority groups attempting to volunteer for service in the armed forces of the United States, Senator Truman voted for an amendment to the Selective Service Act to prevent such discrimination.[9]

In 1942 Mr. Truman signed a cloture petition under Senate Rule XXII to end filibustering against a bill which would have outlawed the use of the poll tax as a prerequisite for voting.[10]

Also in 1942, Senator Truman introduced a bill in Congress to establish the George Washington Carver National Monument, in memory of one of the great Negro scientists of the United States. The purpose of this bill was achieved subsequently with the approval of a House bill having the same objective.[11]

After Mr. Truman succeeded to the presidency of the United States on April 12, 1945, he continued and broadened his support of civil rights. One of his early endeavors was an attempt to have the fair employment practices program of the Federal Government put on a permanent basis.

---

[6]*Congressional Record,* Seventy-fifth Congress, First session. LXXXI, pt. 7, p. 7586.

[7]*Ibid.,* LXXXII, pt. 1, pp. 209-211.

[8]Both times cloture failed to receive a simple majority of votes, let alone the two-thirds majority required. *Ibid.,* LXXXIII, pt. 1, p. 1166, and pt. 2, p. 2007.

[9]*Ibid.,* LXXXVI, pt. 10, p. 10895.

[10]Cloture was defeated in this instance. *Ibid.,* LXXXVIII, pt. 7, p. 9033 and p. 9065.

[11]*Ibid.,* pt. 6, p. 8107, and LXXXIX, pt. 6, p. 2551.

President Roosevelt had established a Fair Employment Practice Committee by Executive order 8802 on June 25, 1941. With the approach of the end of World War II, friends of FEPC desired that the program be authorized by an Act of Congress, to insure its continuation into peacetime. Bills to this effect were introduced into Congress, but they ran into strong opposition.

On June 5, 1945, President Truman wrote a letter to Chairman Adolf J. Sabath of the powerful Rules Committee of the House of Representatives, urging the Rules Committee to expedite consideration of the FEPC bill before it. Among other things, the President stated:

> The principle and policy of fair employment practice should be established permanently as a part of our national law . . . . To abandon at this time the fundamental principle upon which the fair employment practice committee was established is unthinkable. Even if the war were over, or nearly over, the question of fair employment practices during the reconversion period and thereafter would be of paramount importance.
>
> Discrimination in the matter of employment against properly qualified persons because of their race, creed, or color is not only un-American in nature, but will lead eventually to industrial strife and unrest.[12]

In his famous Fair Deal message to Congress on September 6, 1945, President Truman repeated his recommendation for permanent FEPC legislation in these words:

> During the years of war production we made substantial progress in overcoming many of the prejudices which had resulted in discrimination against minority groups.
>
> Many of the injustices based upon considerations of race, religion, and color were removed. Many were prevented. Perfection was not reached, of course, but substantial progress was made.
>
> In the reconversion period and thereafter, we should make every effort to continue this American ideal. It is one of the fundamentals of our political philosophy, and it should be an integral part of our economy.
>
> The Fair Employment Practice Committee is continuing during the transition period. I have already requested that legislation be enacted placing the Fair Employment Practice Committee on a permanent basis. I repeat that recommendation.[13]

When there appeared to be little hope that the Congress would enact the recommended legislation for a permanent FEPC, President Truman issued an Executive order on December 20, 1945, continuing the work of the Fair Employment Practice Committee under the National War Agencies Appropriation Act, 1946. This extended FEPC through June 30, 1946, whereupon it expired for want of further

---

[12]*New York Times,* June 6, 1945, p. 23, col. 8.

[13]*Congressional Record,* Seventy-ninth Congress, First session, LXXXXI, pt. 6, p. 8381.

Congressional authorization. Even before its expiration, FEPC had been greatly crippled because of a lack of adequate appropriations.

At the same time that President Truman issued the Executive order continuing the Fair Employment Practice Committee, he sent a directive to the heads of all United States goverment departments, agencies, and independent establishments, noting "that a considerable number of loyal and qualified employees have been refused transfer and reemployment by employing agencies solely because of race and creed" and requesting "that you make careful analysis of your personnel policies, procedures, and practices in order that you can assure me that they are in accord with national law and policy, and in order that all qualified workers in existing temporary war jobs will be considered fairly for appointment without distinction because of race, creed, color, or national origin. In addition, your full cooperation with FEPC in all matters affecting the employment of minorities in Government is requested."[14]

On December 5, 1946, President Truman took one of the most important steps in his continuing fight for freedom and equality. On that day, by Executive Order, he established the President's Committee on Civil Rights. This distinguished committee, under the Chairmanship of Mr. Charles E. Wilson, former President of General Electric and former War Production Board executive, was "authorized on behalf of the President to inquire into and to determine whether and in what respect current law-enforcement measures and the authority and means possessed by Federal, State and local governments may be strengthened and improved to safeguard the civil rights of the people." Further, the Committee was directed to "make a report of its studies to the President in writing, and shall in particular make recommendations with respect to the adoption or establishment, by legislation or otherwise, of more adequate and effective means and procedures for the protection of the civil rights of the people of the United States."[15]

The President's Committee on Civil Rights presented its written report entitled *To Secure These Rights* in October, 1947. It was published by the Government Printing Office in paperback and contained some 178 pages. Even now—more than a decade after its publication—this report deserves reading or re-reading by every adult American.

---

[14]*Ibid.*, pt. 9, p. 12503 and p. 12505.
[15]Executive Order 9809, December 5, 1946, in *To Secure These Rights: The Report of the President's Committee on Civil Rights*, (Washington, 1947), p. viii.

In four chapters the Committee summed up its findings and recommendations.

In Chapter I, "The American Heritage: The Promise of Freedom and Equality," the Committee restated under four headings the ideals of civil rights upon which this nation was founded: (1) The Right to Safety and Security of the Person; (2) The Right to Citizenship and Its Privileges; (3) The Right to Freedom of Conscience and Expression; and (4) The Right to Equality of Opportunity.

In Chapter II, the Committee on Civil Rights looked the facts squarely in the face and came up with its blunt conclusion, "The Record: Short of the Goal." While recognizing that our diverse population presented some special problems in the way of numerous minorities and while noting with satisfaction that much progress had been made toward greater enjoyment of freedom and equality in the United States, the Committee cited many specific instances where we had failed to attain even a reasonable approximation of the achievement of the four rights set forth in Chapter I of their Report. Included were examples of lynchings, police brutality, faulty administration of justice, involuntary servitude, and harsh treatment of Japanese Americans in World War II. Specific instances where citizenship, the right to vote, and the right to bear arms without discrimination were being unfairly denied to individuals and groups were also cited. The Committee found that the most immediate threat to the right to freedom of conscience and expression was indirect, a by-product, as it were, of the effort "to deal with those few people in our midst who would destroy democracy," the Communists and the native Fascists. The Committee foresaw the danger of "Red hunting" among the civil servants of the Government and counseled, in the words of Justice Brandeis, "the exercise of good judgment" wherein "calmness is, in time of deep feeling and on subjects which excite passion, as essential as fearlessness and honesty."[16]

The right to equality of opportunity, the Committee found, was seriously unattained in employment practices, in education, in housing, in health services, and in other public services and accommodations. The Committee called for an end to segregation and to the "separate but equal doctrine," some six and one-half years before the Supreme Court of the United States took this step in the now famous segregation cases decided on May 17, 1954.[17] Special emphasis was given by the

---

[16]*Ibid.*, p. 49.
[17]*Brown vs. Board of Education of Topeka*, 349 U.S. 294.

Committee to discrimination found in the nation's Capital, a situation which it *"feels most deeply . . . is intolerable."*[18]

"The National Government of the United States," the Committee stated in Chapter III of its Report, "must take the lead in safeguarding the civil rights of all Americans."[19] Among the reasons supporting this conclusion were the inability or unwillingness of state and local governments to do the job, the desirability of using the idealism and prestige of the nation as a whole "to check the wayward tendencies of a part of them,"[20] the growing international implications of our civil rights record, and the popular demand for leadership in civil rights by the national government in its direct dealings with millions of persons as employer and otherwise.

The Civil Rights Committee found that the National Government had the necessary constitutional authority to exercise leadership in the area of civil rights and surveyed briefly the roles of the Supreme Court and of the Department of Justice as guardians of civil rights. In this connection the Committee called attention to the problem of sanctions for enforcing protection of civil rights, such as criminal penalties, civil remedies, administrative orders, grants-in-aid conditioned upon nondiscrimination, and disclosure. The Committee also stressed the basic importance of the climate of public opinion—"a climate of opinion as free from prejudice as we can make it."[21]

In Chapter IV of its Report, the President's Committee on Civil Rights presented its "Program for Action." Stressing that "the time is now," the Committee saw three important reasons for making a sustained drive forward in order to overcome our deficiencies in the civil rights area: (1) The moral reason (*"The United States can no longer countenance these burdens on its common conscience, these inroads on its moral fiber."*) (2) The economic reason (*"The United States can no longer afford this heavy drain upon its human wealth, its national competence."*) (3) The international reason (*"The United States is not so strong, the final triumph of the democratic ideal is not so inevitable that we can ignore what the world thinks of us or our record."*)[22]

The specific recommendations of the Committee were directed toward strengthening the machinery for the protection of civil rights,

---

[18] *To Secure These Rights*, p. 95. Italics in the original.
[19] *Ibid.*, p. 99.
[20] *Ibid.*, p. 100.
[21] *Ibid.*, p. 133.
[22] *Ibid.*, p. 141, p. 146, and p. 148. Italics in the original.

toward strengthening the laws embodying the civil rights, and toward rallying the American people to the support of a continuing program to strengthen civil rights.[23]

On the basis of his Committee's report and recommendations, President Truman sent a special message to the Congress on February 2, 1948, presenting his famous civil rights program. This message is included in this volume as Chapter II. It will be noted that the ten recommendations made by President Truman to the Congress in this message (see page 11) are based directly on the recommendations of his Committee on Civil Rights.

Probably few, if any, Presidential recommendations to the Congress in recent decades have created such a stir or aroused such a storm of opposition as did these civil rights recommendations made by President Truman. The reaction from the South was quick and bitter. Southern members of the House and Senate charged that the President's civil rights program was Communist-inspired and designed to appeal to the Negro vote in the large northern cities—a vote which might be pivotal in the approaching presidential election.[24] The Dixie-crat revolt, which later materialized into support of the candidacy of Strom Thurmond, was predicted at this time.[25]

Opposition to certain parts of President Truman's civil rights program came from places outside the South. For instance, the recommendation of a federal anti-lynching bill was criticized, in an editorial in the *Washington Post*, largely on the grounds of not being necessary, since lynchings had already been reduced to practically zero.[26]

The *New York Times* doubted editorially that a Federal law could "force the FEPC ideal on communities in which majority opinion ran otherwise," and suggested that "a Federal FEPC with power to investigate, recommend and conciliate but no power to enforce might get further than one with a policeman's club."[27]

One representative in Congress who had been for some time an advocate of reform of the electoral college system saw a connection between this system and President Truman's stand on civil rights:

---

[23]*Ibid.*, pp. 151-173, for detailed recommendations.

[24]For sample expressions of extreme southern views, see the remarks of Senator O'Daniel of Texas in the Senate, February 5, 1948, and of Representative Williams of Mississippi in the House of Representatives, February 12, 1948, *Congressional Record*, Eightieth Congress, Second session, LXXXXIV, pt. 1, p. 1120 and p. 1297.

[25]*Ibid.*, remarks of Representative Williams.

[26]*Ibid.*, pt. 2, p. 1987.

[27]*New York Times*, February 22, 1948, p. 24.

It is a form of political expediency or hypocrisy induced by the electoral-college system of choosing Presidents.

Under the archaic, undemocratic system of electing Presidents we have, as a matter of fact, turned over the national politics of the country to two major cities—New York and Chicago. Both parties get down on their bellies and crawl in the dirt and kiss the feet of the organized minorities in the big pivotal States.[28]

President Truman's candidacy for nomination for the Presidency was announced early in March, 1948, and his friends and supporters praised his stand on civil rights as a courageous one, since it might cost him part or all of the South.[29]

The Democratic National Convention which nominated President Truman for the Presidency in 1948 also adopted a platform containing strong and detailed civil rights planks, and this made certain the Dixiecrat walkout.

The Congress had taken no action on President Truman's civil rights recommendations when it adjourned before the national conventions met. President Truman dramatically announced in his acceptance speech before the Democratic National Convention that he was calling the Congress back into special session on July 26, 1948. This was the Republican Eightieth Congress, and the President indicated that he was going to give them a chance to make good on their platform pledges right away. On the very day the special session convened, the President issued two executive orders, one establishing a fair employment practices program for Federal employees, the other abolishing segregation in the armed forces. In his message to the special session of the Congress, President Truman stated: "Finally, I wish again to urge upon the Congress the measures I recommended last February to protect and extend basic civil rights of citizenship and human liberty."[30]

The Congress, however, continued to maintain a completely negative record on civil rights and adjourned without taking any positive steps in this area.

Following his startling victory at the polls in November, 1948, President Truman renewed his efforts to secure civil rights legislation in these words to the new Eighty-first Congress:

[28]From the remarks of Representative Gossett of Texas in the House of Representatives, February 3, 1948. *Congressional Record,* LXXXIV, pt. 1, p. 976.

[29]See, for example, the speech by Senator J. Howard McGrath, Chairman of the Democratic National Committee, reprinted in the *Congressional Record,* LXXXXIV, pt. 10, p. A1568.

[30]*Ibid.,* LXXXIV, pt. 8, p. 9442.

We believe that no unfair prejudice or artificial distinction should bar any citizen of the United States from an education, or from good health, or from a job that he is capable of performing.

The driving force behind our progress is our faith in our democratic institutions. That faith is embodied in the promise of equal rights and equal opportunities which the founders of our Republic proclaimed to their countrymen and to the whole world.

The fulfillment of this promise is among the highest purposes of government. The civil rights proposals I made to the Eightieth Congress, I now repeat to the Eighty-first Congress. They should be enacted in order that the Federal Government may assume the leadership and discharge the obligations clearly placed upon it by the Constitution.

I stand squarely behind these proposals.[31]

Although several bills were introduced in the Eighty-first Congress to carry out the President's civil rights recommendations, none of these bills became law.

In his annual message of January 4, 1950, President Truman pleaded again for enactment of the civil rights proposals which he had made on February 2, 1948, but again he ran into a stone wall of opposition, particularly from the South.

The Eighty-second Congress in 1951 and 1952, absorbed in the problems of the Korean conflict, gave even less attention to civil rights than had the preceding Congress. President Truman pointed out to this Congress in his annual message of January 9, 1952, that "The executive branch has been making real progress toward full equality of treatment and opportunity—in the Armed Forces, in the civil service, and in private firms working for the Government. Further advances require action by the Congress, and I hope that means will be provided to give the Members of the Senate and the House a chance to vote on them."[32]

In reviewing the record on civil rights during and since World War II, President Truman, in his last annual message to Congress, January 7, 1953, stated:

During the war we achieved great economic and social gains for millions of our fellow citizens who had been held back by prejudice. Were we prepared, in peacetime, to keep on moving toward full realization of the democratic promise? Or would we let it be submerged, wiped out, in postwar riots and reaction, as after World War I?

We answered these questions in a series of forward steps at every level of government and in many spheres of private life. In our Armed Forces, our civil service, our universities, our railway trains, the residential districts of our cities—in stores and factories all across the nation—in

---

[31]*Ibid.*, LXXXXV, pt. 1, p. 76.
[32]*Ibid.*, LXXXXVIII, pt. 1, p. 34.

the polling booths as well—the barriers are coming down. This is happening, in part, at the mandate of the courts; in part, at the insistence of Federal, State, and local governments; in part, through the enlightened action of private groups and persons in every region and every walk of life.

There has been a great awakening of the American conscience on the issues of civil rights. And all this progress—still far from complete but still continuing—has been our answer, up to now, to those who questioned our intention to live up to the promises of equal freedom for us all.[33]

President Truman's high regard for equality is further illustrated in his veto message on the Immigration and Naturalization Act of 1952, presented in Chapter IX of this volume. Although himself descended from the dominant northern and western European nationality groups in the United States, President Truman not only vetoed this piece of legislation but followed it up with the appointment of the President's Commission on Immigration and Naturalization which presented a very liberal report urging sweeping revision of the law which had been passed over the President's veto.

This seven-member Commission, whose chairman was Philip B. Perlman, stated that our immigration and nationality law should perform two functions: "First, it should regulate the admission and naturalization of aliens in the best interests of the United States. Second, it should properly reflect the traditions and fundamental ideals of the American people in determining 'whom we shall welcome to a participation of all our rights and privileges'."

The traditions and fundamental ideals of the American people were stated by the Commission as follows:

1. *America was founded upon the principle that all men are created equal, that the differences of race, color, religion, or national origin should not be used to deny equal treatment or equal opportunity* . . . .

2. *America historically has been the haven for the oppressed of other lands* . . . .

3. *American national unity has been achieved without national uniformity* . . . .

4. *Americans have believed in fair treatment for all* . . . .

5. *America's philosophy has always been one of faith in our future and belief in progress* . . . .

6. *American foreign policy seeks peace and freedom, mutual understanding and a high standard of living for ourselves and our world neighbors* . . . .

After finding that our present immigration laws "flout fundamental American traditions and ideals," the Commission urged that these laws be completely rewritten.

---

[33]*Ibid.*, LXXXXIX, pt. 1, p. 236.

Among the seventeen specific recommendations of the Commissions were the following:

1. The national origins quota system should be abolished.
2. There should be a unified quota system, which would allocate visas without regard to national origin, race, creed, or color.
3. The maximum annual quota immigration should be one-sixth of one per cent of the population of the United States, as determined by the most recent census. Under the 1950 census, quota immigration would be open to 251,162 immigrants annually, instead of the 154,657 now authorized.

Other recommendations of the Commission favored creation of a new independent agency to administer the law; the establishment of specific country quotas by this agency on the basis of five categories; the right of asylum, reunion of families, needs in the United States, special needs in the free world, and general immigration.

The Commission also made recommendations *re* fair hearings and procedures, bases for admissions and deportations, safeguarding of the security of the United States, and equalizing of the status of naturalized citizens with that of native-born citizens.[34]

By the time the Report of this Commission was available, January 1, 1953, the inauguration of a new President was less than three weeks away. The impact of the Report was thus largely lost in the commotion caused by the changing of regimes.

How President Truman's fight for equality is evaluated depends largely upon the point of view of the one making the evaluation. As we have seen, his Civil Rights Message of February 2, 1948, was bitterly denounced by its opponents as a vote-catching device, full of hypocrisy and deceit. Friends of the program were just as warm in their praise of it as an example of courageous leadership, embodying the noblest ideals of American democracy.

The political analyst can perhaps detect in Mr. Truman's civil rights program a happy union of idealism and realism—those twin touchstones which a political leader ignores at his peril. The ideal of equality, enshrined in one of the great documents of human history— the American Declaration of Independence—in the immortal words of Thomas Jefferson, "All men are created equal," has exerted a powerful influence upon American political thought and action. No modern American political leader dare reject it.

---

[34]The source of this summary is the *Department of State Bulletin*, January 19, 1953, XXVIII, pp. 97-102. Italics in the original.

At the same time there has appeared in twentieth-century America what Samuel Lubell has called the "urban frontier" with its "civil rights melting pot," consisting not only of Negroes but of many other religious and national minority groups. These groups must be taken into account by anyone hoping to achieve a successful coalition in American national politics today. (See Samuel Lubell, *The Future of American Politics*, Doubleday Anchor book, 1956, especially chapters 3-5, inclusive.)

It was peculiarly fitting, therefore, that Harry S. Truman, combining a keen appreciation of the traditional ideals of American history with a shrewd understanding of practical politics, should have championed a civil rights program that embodied both the ideal and the real. Never before in American history had a President of the United States attempted in a period of foreign stress to carry forward such a significant program of progressive reform in domestic affairs.

Mr. Truman on Freedom

Throughout his almost eight years in the White House, Mr. Truman had to wrestle with the threat of Communism at home as well as abroad. While he was determined to combat the Communist menace, he was also resolute in his conviction that we should not destroy freedom in the process of defending it. He therefore took a clear and unequivocal stand against McCarthyism and in favor of the Bill of Rights.

The nub of this question was how to combat Communism without crippling the Constitution. The problem broke down into three parts: (1) how to prevent Communists from getting into the government service, especially in sensitive areas, and how to get them out if they did get in; (2) how to keep classified information out of the hands of the Communists; and (3) how to control Communists and Communist activity in general.

Getting Communists out of the government had received much attention from the House Un-American Activities Committee before Truman became President, but many liberals thought that individual rights were too often sacrificed by this Committee upon the altar of political publicity. To protect the rights of individuals without sacrificing the security of the government, President Truman created a loyalty system under Executive Order 9835 on March 21, 1947. This order established agency loyalty boards to pass upon the loyalty of persons already in the Federal civil service and regional loyalty boards

throughout the United States to pass upon the loyalty of persons
applying for positions in the Federal civil service. A Loyalty Review
Board under the Civil Service Commission was established to hear
appeals brought from the decisions of agency and regional boards.

The executive Order of March 21, 1948, defined the main criterion
for loyalty board decisions as follows: "The standard for the refusal
of employment or the removal from employment . . . shall be that . . .
reasonable grounds exist for belief that the person involved is disloyal to the Government of the United States." Further, the Executive
Order stated that "activities and associations of an . . . employee
which may be considered in connection with the determination of
disloyalty may include one or more of the following: . . . membership
in, affiliation with, or sympathetic association with any foreign or
domestic organization, association, movement, group, or combination
of persons; designated by the Attorney General as totalitarian, Fascist,
Communist, or subversive, or as having adopted a policy of advocating
or approving the commission of acts of force or violence to deny other
persons their rights under the Constitution of the United States, or as
seeking to alter the form of government of the United States by unconstitutional means."

President Truman's loyalty-check program was immediately attacked by liberals on both substantive and procedural grounds, although
some of them recognized that in the final analysis much would depend
upon the manner in which the program was administered.[35]

Criticism from the right also came immediately, and it was more
persistent, because the actual administration of the loyalty program
under Mr. Seth Richardson, Chairman of the Loyalty Review Board,
embodied an essentially liberal spirit.[36]

The liberal emphasis in the loyalty-check program was maintained
even during the period of McCarthyism. President Truman, however,
did tighten his program somewhat by amending his Executive Order

[35]See, for example, the letter of April 10, 1947, to the *New York Times*,
April 13, 1947, from a group of professors of the Harvard Law School, namely,
Zechariah Chafee, Jr., Erwin N. Griswold, Milton Katz, and Austin W. Scott,
reprinted in the *Congressional Record*, LXXXXIII, pt. 11, pp. A1763-1764. See
also the remarks of Representative Chet Hollifield in the House of Representatives,
ibid., pt. 6, p. 7847.

[36]For example, see the remarks of Representative Busbey, *Congressional Record*,
LXXXXIV, pt. 10, p. A2530; of Senator Ferguson, *ibid.*, LXXXXVII, pt. 1,
p. 1145; and of Representative Velde, *ibid.*, pt. 4, p. 4759.

of March 21, 1947, to afford less protection to the individual and more to the Government, as follows: "The standard for the refusal of employment or the removal from employment in an executive department or agency on grounds relating to loyalty shall be that, on all the evidence, there is a reasonable doubt as to the loyalty of the person involved to the Government of the United States."

The administration of the loyalty-check program was not accomplished without clashes between the Executive Branch and the Congress. Some of these clashes were over the refusal of the President to allow records, reports, and files relative to the loyalty program to be turned over to members or committees of Congress without the approval of his office in each particular case.[37]

This issue became particularly acute when the House Un-American Activities Committee demanded that the Executive Branch turn over to them a letter from J. Edgar Hoover, Director of the Federal Bureau of Investigation, to W. Averell Harriman, Secretary of Commerce, concerning Dr. Edward U. Condon, Director of the Bureau of Standards.[38] Under direct orders from the President, Secretary Harriman refused to comply with this demand. The confidential nature of employee loyalty records was thus maintained, in the face of a resolution adopted by the House of Representatives "that the Secretary of Commerce is hereby directed to transmit forthwith to the House of Representatives the full text of a letter dated May 15, 1947."[39]

The problem of keeping Communists and other disloyal persons out of the Government service or of removing them if in the Government service was only one by-product of the cold war between Russia and the United States. Another, closely related, was that of preventing

---

[37]The text of President Truman's directive, "Confidential Status of Employee Loyalty Records," March 13, 1948, may be found in *Congressional Record*, LXXXXIV, pt. 3, p. 2929.

[38]*Ibid.*, LXXXXIV, pt. 4, pp. 4777 *et seq.*

[39]One representative, speaking for the resolution, made the following statement: "As further background to the information contained in the letter of J. Edgar Hoover, and which makes it highly necessary for the Committee on Un-American Activities to have possession of the full contents of the letter, is the allegation that Dr. Condon has made a number of speeches indicating an interest in Russia . . . ." *Congressional Record*, LXXXXIV, pt. 4, p. 4778.

It is beyond the scope of this brief chapter to attempt to give a detailed account of the loyalty-check program under President Truman. An excellent bibliography on this and related subjects may be found in John W. Caughey, *In Clear and Present Danger* (Chicago, 1958), pp. 193-202.

classified information from getting out of the Government and into the hands of actual or potential enemies. To help prevent the divulging of classified information by departments and agencies of the executive branch, President Truman issued Executive Order 10290 on September 24, 1951. This order actually extended the existing rules and regulations concerning the handling of classified material in the Departments of Defense and State and in the Atomic Energy Commission to all the rest of the Executive Branch.

Some of the same Senators who had been the most vocal critics of the Truman administration for alleged laxity in dealing with the Communist problem criticized this Executive Order on the grounds that it interferred with freedom of the press.[40] Well could the President have concluded that he was bound to be damned if he did and damned if he didn't.

The third and final aspect of the Communist problem within the United States with which President Truman had to wrestle was the broad one of how to cope with the Communist threat in general, aside from infiltration into the government service and aside from gaining access to security secrets. How much freedom should the Communists enjoy in pursuing their political activities? Should the Communist Party in effect be outlawed?

President Truman's views on these and similar questions are given in his speeches and messages to Congress presented in Chapter IV through IX in this volume. He wisely perceived that constructive action "to improve the standard of living of our people, to assure equal opportunity for all, to promote their health and education, and their security and freedom" was one of the best ways to head off the Communists. At the same time, President Truman used the Smith Act and other laws on the statute books to prosecute the Communists for subversive activities, "within the framework of the democratic liberties we cherish."

Mr. Truman's attitude and actions concerning the Communists have been criticized from both the left and right. Some left-of-center liberals were unhappy with the loyalty program, the control over the release of classified material, and with the Smith Act prosecutions.

On the other hand, conservatives and certain partisan opponents of Mr. Truman indulged in almost completely unrestrained attacks

---

[40]*Congressional Record*, LXXXXVII, pt. 10, p. 12853.

upon him for dealing too gently with the Communists. They made Communism one of the big issues in the 1952 presidential campaign. After the new regime took over in 1953, one Attorney General of the United States even came close to accusing Mr. Truman of treasonable action in allegedly knowingly keeping a Soviet spy in high office— a charge which Mr. Truman answered on radio and television.

Much of the severe criticism from the right could of course be ascribed to partisan motivation; during the period of McCarthy hysteria it was a cheap way to make the headlines. Even the serious and sincere critics of both right and left probably failed to appreciate the problem which faced the man in power—the necessity of striking a balance between freedom and authority. Enjoying the luxury of irresponsibility, they could judge every action by more or less absolute standards (the left, by the standard of freedom of the individual; the right, by the standard of security of the nation). Mr. Truman, as President, had to strike a balance between these two desiderata. This necessarily meant compromise, and compromise is seldom acceptable to extremists, doctrinaires, or idealists who do not have the awful responsibility which goes with power. These persons may make valuable contributions to political life by sharply delineating the possible goals which should be kept in mind, but it is doubtful if they should give the final judgment on what is accomplished in the very practical realm of politics. While the ends may be absolute, the means must always be relative to the circumstances. Politics is still the art of the possible.

It is suggested here that Mr. Truman's record in dealing with the threat of Communism speaks for itself. The significance of this record, with regard to both equality and freedom, should be judged in the light of historical perspective. Often in the past, eras of progressive reform have been swamped in the backwash of war. This was certainly true of Woodrow Wilson's New Freedom, which fell afoul of World War I. That the New Deal-Fair Deal did not suffer a similar fate at the hands of World War II is undoubtedly attributable in large measure to the challenge of Russian and Chinese Communism, which did not allow us the luxury of relaxing in a postwar letdown marked mainly by unmitigated materialism.

For those who believe, however, that the quality of leadership which a nation enjoys is not altogether unimportant in shaping its destiny, it must remain a point that Mr. Truman provided leadership which met the great challenges to freedom and equality. Clinton Rossiter puts it this way: "There appear to have been two great events in Truman's eight years for which he may be remembered as Madison or Grant or Taft or Hoover will never be remembered. One was domestic in character—the first real beginnings of a many-sided program toward eliminating discrimination and second-class citizenship in American life. The other was international—the irrevocable commitment of the American people to active cooperation with other nations in search of world peace and prosperity."[41]

The speeches and state papers which follow deal with the first of those two events.

---

[41]*The American Presidency*, p. 120.

FREEDOM
AND
EQUALITY

CHAPTER I

The New Deal for the Negro

An address delivered by Senator Harry S. Truman to the Convention of the National Colored Democratic Association, July 14, 1940, at the Eighth Regiment Armory, Chicago, Illinois. (From the Appendix to the *Congressional Record*, Seventy-sixth Congress, Third session. LXXXVI, pt. 17, pp. 5367-5369.)

There is much being said these days about the Negro and what should be done with him instead of what should be done for him. Much is written about his rights as a person, but it has been up to the present administration to take the problem in hand and provide necessary measures for his life, liberty, and pursuit of happiness.

That the administration has already done much for the Negro is clearly evidenced by the results of recent elections in such cities as Kansas City, St. Louis, and Chicago. In these and other large cities, the Negro wards showed a much larger proportionate Democratic vote than in the white wards, and to my notion this is as it should be since the Negro race has received treatment at the hands of the present administration that should justify its continued support.

Up until the time of the emancipation, Negroes were in an entirely different status from their fellow men in America. Besides the injustice of enslavement, they were held far beneath the white population in almost every measure of modern civilization. This was anything but a reflection on the ability of the black men. With education positively forbidden to him and the fact that he was forced into a culture, civilization, and climate absolutely new to him, is it any wonder that his progression has been at times a disturbed one? Can any of you picture yourselves planted suddenly in the wilds of Africa and forced to make your own way in a hostile society utterly different from anything you have ever known? That has been the problem of our Negro population.

In the years before the Roosevelt administration, plotting politicians attempted to defeat Negro suffrage which was gained only after the toil and heartbreak of three constitutional amendments. First of all, they imposed a property qualification for the privilege of voting, but the colored people acquired property so rapidly that the politicians were temporarily baffled. It was necessary to resort to other measures. They required educational attainments, but for once the demand was reasonable.

It was a double blessing to the Negro since it opened the way to the polls and inspired the colored people to learn at least the primary requirements of education. It was a wise provision insofar as a certain amount of learning should become a requirement of any American citizen. Of course, this also supposes that the means of education shall be provided. No citizen can fulfill his mission at the ballot box unless he is able to read and write to inform himself about public men and measures. Naturally, the rule should apply to white and black alike. Here was the Negro's big chance to remove the last obstacle between himself and the polls as well as to advance in culture.

Up to the time of the Emancipation, the Negro's slavery forbade him education and kept him in a completely dependent state. During the period of freedom, he was almost equally handicapped. Being under servile conditions for over 300 years, and naturally unused to constructive thinking, how could he be expected to have accomplished more than he has within a single generation? No one could hope that the Negro would become a nation-illuminating legal, industrial, or literary light the day following the Emancipation Proclamation. Notwithstanding, the Negro has done amazingly well.

That old-time slave owner felt that an educated Negro would be a menace. If the slave knew too much it was feared he would learn to revolt and become haughty. We all know that the old-time slave owner was mistaken. The educated Negro learns quickly so that in order to protect himself, he must obey the law, not break it. He can only blunder in performing his civic duties if he does not understand them.

Fear that Negro education may menace the white race's conception of racial safety displays nothing more than a narrow conception of good citizenship and an amazing ignorance of Negro characteristics. Always, it is the uneducated person, regardless of color, who is the dangerous citizen. It is your ignorant class among the people that is the criminal class.

In this light, let us see what the present administration has done for the Negro. As I have stated, it has given him $2,000,000 for improvements at Howard University and Freedman's Hospital; $262,000 to Virginia State College; $87,000 for Lincoln University in Missouri; $500,000 for the Wendell Phillips High School at Chicago; $40,000 for West Virginia State College; paid $100 per month to 114 colored school teachers in Chicago engaged in the work of reducing adult illiteracy, and has extended this benevolent aid in many other directions.

Ignorance breeds all of the festering prejudices of our human family. The fraternizing sentiments of mankind are products of education. In my opinion, greater educational facilities for the Negro would be a blessing to him and at the same time a great boon to society at large. If white men wish to do better for themselves, it would be well for them to give more definite attention to the education of the Negro.

By this I mean not merely more and better buildings and equipment, but very careful attention to what is taught in these buildings. We exert no little care to see what white children are taught in our public schools, but seem to have little or no concern about what the Negro child is taught. Especially now, right teaching on patriotism, morals, and race relationship in our schools, both white and black, is an essential element in any program for the solution of the Negro question. When we are honest enough to recognize each other's rights and are good enough to respect them, we will come to a more Christian settlement of our difficulties. Education of the Negro guarantees safety to the white people and certainly is to their interest. All dark people, except the Negroes, are against the white race.

Some say that the Negro is not capable of assimilating cultural study. I have always denied this and have studied the problem sufficiently to know that given an equal opportunity with white students, the Negro can more than hold his own.

Take for example, the story of Phyllis Wheatly, the first colored American poetess. When she was but 7 years old, she was captured in Africa and sold to a right Boston family named Wheatly. Mrs. Wheatly educated the girl and the development of her mind was phenomenal. This little waif from the African jungle was writing rhymes at 14, at 17 reputable verse, and at 20 published a book of poems. She visited London and was feted by royalty. It was she who originally spoke of George Washington as "first in peace." When Washington died, Congress extended the phrase to read "first in peace, first in war, first in the hearts of his countrymen," but Phyllis Wheatly, who first gave birth to the idea was a Negress. Don't forget, too, that one of the world's foremost agricultural chemists who has done so much for the South is a Negro. George Washington Carver, of Tuskegee Institute, is a Negro and a fellow of the London Royal Society of Arts. He has done more for the welfare and upbuilding of his race than any living person.

I repeat, the Negro needs only the opportunity for cultural study. He has the ability.

Before I go further, I wish to make it clear that I am not appealing for social equality of the Negro. The Negro himself knows better than that, and the highest types of Negro leaders say quite frankly that they prefer the society of their own people. Negroes want justice, not social relations. I merely wish to sound a note of warning. Numberless antagonisms and indignities heaped upon any race will eventually try human patience to the limit and a crisis will develop. We all know the Negro is here to stay and in no way can be removed from our political and economic life and we should recognize his inalienable rights as specified in our Constitution. Can any man claim protection of our laws if he denies that protection to others?

Under the Roosevelt Administration, more has been done to give the Negro equal legal, economic, and cultural rights than has ever been done before. The Honorable John M. Houston, of Kansas, has said that President Roosevelt has appointed more Negroes to responsible governmental positions than the last three Republican administrations combined. While these things are individual honors, the colored people will benefit by the Roosevelt policies. Every law passed by our present Congress for direct relief or otherwise gives the Negro his equal rights. For the first time in our history, the administration has given us a colored man in the White House on the secretarial staff. This is absolutely unprecedented.

The colored man was taught through the years that the Republican Party, and that party alone, freed him from slavery. Naturally he felt grateful to that party and thought it no more than right that he should vote for it. He knows now that from the Civil War until the present administration he has been exploited by the Republican Party. During the campaigns, of course, the Republican candidates were the friend of the Negro and his greatest benefactor. Between campaigns, however, these fine "friends" forgot the Negro.

As the generations of Negroes went on and became better educated they began to sense that something was wrong. They began to
wonder if their race still owed a "debt of gratitude" to a party which
did nothing for them except in election year. Finally the Negro voters
realized that with the Republican Party it was all "take" and no
"give." In short, what the Negro was fighting for was his constitutional right of equal opportunity under law for himself and his children.
He needed a redeal in the game of life.

That he got it, no one will or can deny. Doctor Thompkins,
Recorder of Deeds of the District of Columbia, has said: "The administration has given us representation as economists in National
Recovery Administration. It has given us several architects and engi-
neers in the Subsistence Homestead Division of the NRA. It has given
us representation on the legal staff of the Public Works Administration
and in the Post Office Department; it has given us a representative in
the Farm Credit Bureau of the Agricultural Adjustment Administration
to look after the needs and opportunities of the colored farmers of
the country; it has given us a clearing house in the Department of
Interior, presided over by a highly efficient representative of the race,
assisted by a competent staff to promote the economic status of the
race; it has given us representation in the vast welfare operations of
the WPA under Colonel Harrington; it has given us significant representation in the Department of Justice and in the Office of the Recorder
of Deeds of the District of Columbia; it gave us our first Federal
judge in the person of William H. Hastie, and upon his resignation,
Attorney Moore, of Chicago, was appointed as his successor; it has
given us 25 outstanding high-salaried posts of distinction, including
representation among the conciliators of the Department of Labor, and
an adviser to the Secretary of Commerce on racial matters."

Who can look upon a record so humane and just and not thrill
with pride at the very mention of the President and his entire administration?

The administration has also undertaken a far-reaching program
of slum clearance to better the wretched living conditions of thousands
of Negro families. I believe, and I think you will all agree, that one
of the prime requisites of a sound democracy is good housing.

We must not forget that every community owes the Negro a fair
deal in regard to public utilities, lights, and sewers, street improvement,
and water mains. We owe the Negro legal equality and a fair chance in

the world for several reasons, not in the least of them because he is a human being and a natural-born American. Because his political power is yet weak, he cannot be denied his rights. Never must we forget that if we sink the Negro to the depths of hopeless degradation and make no provision for his comfort in housing or any other necessity of life, the law of compensation will take effect and the whites, too, will go down with him.

The famous Booker T. Washington often said, "You cannot hold a Negro in the gutter unless some white man stays in the gutter to hold him there."

The housing project of the administration will not hold the Negro in the "gutter" but instead will remove him and the "gutter" too.

The final result of its program will be to provide modern, comfortable dwellings for these thousands of families so that their children may grow up to love their country in a decent environment with the modern conveniences and playground facilities so necessary to a happy and healthful life. And whenever it is possible, Negro managers will be employed in the housing projects tenanted mainly by colored people. Although our work has just begun, already we have completed or are working on, projects in such cities as Atlanta, St. Louis, Kansas City, Chicago, New York, Nashville, New Orleans, and others. Compare empty platform promises of the Republican Party with the real achievements of our administration and you cannot fail to see that the New Deal is the hope of the Negro as well as every other group or class in these United States.

That the Negro is entitled to every right under law is sometimes contested on the very weak grounds that he had no worthy part in American history. Turn to your histories then, and you will see the record of patriotism the colored man has written for himself in the pages of our Nation's development. The first American Negro to give up his life for our country's liberty was Crispus Attucks who was shot down in the Boston massacre of 1770. A Negro, Peter Salem, was the hero of the Battle of Bunker Hill and is credited with the death of the British commander, Major Pitcairn.

Gen. Andrew Jackson, in speaking to the Negroes after the Battle of New Orleans, said, "To the men of color—soldiers from the shores of Mobile I collected you to arms. I invited you to share in the perils and divide the glory of your white countrymen. I expected much of you but you surpass my hopes—the President of the United States shall be informed of your conduct on the present occasion and the voice of the representatives of the American Nation shall applaud your valor, as your general now praises your ardor."

Commodore Perry spoke in high praise of his Negro sailors in the Battle of Lake Erie. Negroes distinguished themselves in the Spanish-American War at the battles of Guasimas, El Caney, and San Juan Hill.

In the World War, four entire Negro regiments received the coveted Croix de Guerre for heroism in action. Gen. John J. Pershing said of the Negroes' World War record: "The only regret expressed by colored troops is that they are not given more dangerous work to do. I cannot commend too highly the spirit shown among the colored combat troups, who exhibit fine capacity for quick training and eagerness for the most dangerous work." The Negroes' flag is our flag, and he stands ready, just as we do, to defend it against all foes from within and without.

The Negro wants love, not compassion; human understanding, not abstract resolutions. He wants to be helped, not crushed. He wants opportunities to better himself, not relief. He wants just wages, not alms. He wants stability, security, and friendliness. He knows that the Roosevelt administration has been his salvation in these days of turmoil, strife, and depression.

He must not switch now from the Democratic Party, which has done so much for him and will ever continue to work in his best interests. He must not switch from the party which embodies every ideal upon which this country has been built to a party which thrives only on broken promises.

We must all love, honor, and serve our country together.

This can be done successfully only under the Democratic Party.

Thank you.

CHAPTER II

Civil Rights Message

A Message to the Congress of the United States from President Harry S. Truman, February 2, 1948. (From the *Congressional Record*, Eightieth Congress, Second session. LXXXXIV, pt. 1, pp. 927-929.)

To the Congress of the United States:

In the state of the Union message on January 7, 1948, I spoke of five great goals toward which we should strive in our constant effort to strengthen our democracy and improve the welfare of our people. The first of these is to secure fully our essential human rights. I am now presenting to the Congress my recommendations for legislation to carry us forward toward that goal.

This Nation was founded by men and women who sought these shores that they might enjoy greater freedom and greater opportunity than they had known before. The founders of the United States proclaimed to the world the American belief that all men are created equal, and that governments are instituted to secure the inalienable rights with which all men are endowed. In the Declaration of Independence and the Constitution of the United States, they eloquently expressed the aspirations of all mankind for equality and freedom.

These ideals inspired the peoples of other lands, and their practical fulfillment made the United States the hope of the oppressed everywhere. Throughout our history men and women of all colors and creeds, of all races and religions, have come to this country to escape tyranny and discrimination. Millions strong, they have helped build this democratic Nation and have constantly reinforced our devotion to the great ideals of liberty and equality. With those who preceded them, they have helped to fashion and strengthen our American faith —a faith that can be simply stated:

We believe that all men are created equal and that they have the right to equal justice under law.

We believe that all men have the right to freedom of thought and of expression and the right to worship as they please.

We believe that all men are entitled to equal opportunities for jobs, for homes, for good health, and for education.

We believe that all men should have a voice in their Government and that Government should protect, not usurp, the rights of the people.

These are the basic civil rights which are the source and the support of our democracy.

Today, the American people enjoy more freedom and opportunity than ever before. Never in our history has there been better reason to hope for the complete realization of the ideals of liberty and equality.

We shall not, however, finally achieve the ideals for which this Nation was founded so long as any American suffers discrimination as a result of his race, or religion, or color, or the land of origin of his forefathers.

Unfortunately, there still are examples — flagrant examples — of discrimination which are utterly contrary to our ideals. Not all groups of our population are free from the fear of violence. Not all groups are free to live and work where they please or to improve their conditions of life by their own efforts. Not all groups enjoy the full privileges of citizenship and participation in the government under which they live.

We cannot be satisfied until all our people have equal opportunities for jobs, for homes, for education, for health, and for political expression, and until all our people have equal protection under the law.

One year ago I appointed a committee of 15 distinguished Americans and asked them to appraise the condition of our civil rights and to recommend appropriate action by Federal, State, and local governments.

The committee's appraisal has resulted in a frank and revealing report. This report emphasizes that our basic human freedoms are better cared for and more vigilantly defended than ever before. But it also makes clear that there is a serious gap between our ideals and some of our practices. This gap must be closed.

This will take the strong efforts of each of us individually, and all of us acting together through voluntary organizations and our governments.

The protection of civil rights begins with the mutual respect for the rights of others which all of us should practice in our daily lives. Through organizations in every community—in all parts of the country —we must continue to develop practical, workable arrangements for achieving greater tolerance and brotherhood.

The protection of civil rights is the duty of every government which derives its powers from the consent of the people. This is usually true of local, State, and national governments. There is much that the States can and should do at this time to extend their protection of civil rights. Wherever the law enforcement measures of State and local governments are inadequate to discharge this primary function of government, these measures should be strengthened and improved.

The Federal Government has a clear duty to see that constitutional guaranties of individual liberties and of equal protection under the laws are not denied or abridged anywhere in our Union. That duty is shared by all three branches of the Government, but it can be fulfilled only if the Congress enacts modern, comprehensive civil-rights laws, adequate to the needs of the day, and demonstrating our continuing faith in the free way of life.

I recommend, therefore, that the Congress enact legislation at this session directed toward the following specific objectives:

1. Establishing a permanent Commission on Civil Rights, a Joint Congressional Committee on Civil Rights, and a Civil Rights Division in the Department of Justice.

2. Strengthening existing civil-rights statutes.

3. Providing Federal protection against lynching.

4. Protecting more adequately the right to vote.

5. Establishing a Fair Employment Practice Commission to prevent unfair discrimination in employment.

6. Prohibiting discrimination in interstate transportation facilities.

7. Providing home rule and suffrage in Presidential elections for the residents of the District of Columbia.

8. Providing statehood for Hawaii and Alaska and a greater measure of self-government for our island possessions.

9. Equalizing the opportunities for residents of the United States to become naturalized citizens.

10. Settling the evacuation claims of Japanese-Americans.

Strengthening the Government Organization

As a first step, we must strengthen the organization of the Federal Government in order to enforce civil-rights legislation more adequately and to watch over the state of our traditional liberties.

I recommend that the Congress establish a permanent Commission on Civil Rights reporting to the President. The Commission should continuously review our civil-rights policies and practices, study specific problems, and make recommendations to the President at frequent intervals. It should work with other agencies of the Federal Government, with State and local governments, and with private organizations.

I also suggest that the Congress establish a Joint Congressional Committee on Civil Rights. This committee should make a continuing study of legislative matters relating to civil rights and should consider means of improving respect for and enforcement of those rights.

These two bodies together should keep all of us continuously aware of the condition of civil rights in the United States and keep us alert to opportunities to improve their protection.

To provide for better enforcement of Federal civil rights laws there will be established a Division of Civil Rights in the Department of Justice. I recommend that the Congress provide for an additional Assistant Attorney General to supervise this Division.

Strengthening Existing Civil-Rights Statutes

I recommend that the Congress amend and strengthen the existing provisions of Federal law which safeguard the right to vote and the right to safety and security of person and property. These provisions are the basis for our present civil-rights enforcement program.

Section 51 of title 18 of the United States Code, which now gives protection to citizens in the enjoyment of rights secured by the Constitution or Federal laws, needs to be strengthened in two respects. In its present form this section protects persons only if they are citizens, and it affords protection only against conspiracies by two or more persons. This protection should be extended to all inhabitants of the United States, whether or not they are citizens, and should be afforded against infringement by persons acting individually as well as in conspiracy.

Section 52 of title 18 of the United States Code, which now gives general protection to individuals against the deprivation of federally secured rights by public officers, has proved to be inadequate in some cases because of the generality of its language. An enumeration of the principal rights protected under this section is needed to make more definite and certain the protection which the section affords.

Federal Protection Against Lynching

A specific Federal measure is needed to deal with the crime of lynching—against which I cannot speak too strongly. It is a principle of our democracy, written into our Constitution, that every person accused of an offense against the law shall have a fair, orderly trial in an impartial court. We have made great progress toward this end, but I regret to say that lynching has not yet finally disappeared from our land. So long as one person walks in fear of lynching, we shall not have achieved equal justice under law. I call upon the Congress to take decisive action against this crime.

Protecting the Right to Vote

Under the Constitution, the right of all properly qualified citizens to vote is beyond question. Yet the exercise of this right is still subject to interference. Some individuals are prevented from voting by isolated acts of intimidation. Some whole groups are prevented by outmoded policies prevailing in certain States or communities.

We need stronger statutory protection of the right to vote. I urge the Congress to enact legislation forbidding interference by public officers or private persons with the right of qualified citizens to participate in primary, special, and general elections in which Federal officers are to be chosen. This legislation should extend to elections for State as well as Federal officers insofar as interference with the right to vote results from discriminatory action by public officers based on race, color, or other unreasonable classification.

Requirements for the payment of poll taxes also interfere with the right to vote. There are still seven States which, by their constitutions, place this barrier between their citizens and the ballot box. The American people would welcome voluntary action on the part of these States to remove this barrier. Nevertheless, I believe the Congress should enact measures insuring that the right to vote in elections for Federal officers shall not be contingent upon the payment of taxes.

I wish to make it clear that the enactment of the measures I have recommended will in no sense result in Federal conduct of elections. They are designed to give qualified citizens Federal protection of their right to vote. The actual conduct of elections, as always, will remain the responsibility of State governments.

Fair Employment Practice Commission

We in the United States believe that all men are entitled to equality of opportunity. Racial, religious, and other invidious forms of discrimination deprive the individual of an equal chance to develop and utilize his talents and to enjoy the rewards of his efforts.

Once more I repeat my request that the Congress enact fair employment practice legislation prohibiting discrimination in employment based on race, color, religion, or national origin. The legislation should create a Fair Employment Practice Commission with authority to prevent discrimination by employers and labor unions, trade and professional associations, and Government agencies and employment bureaus. The degree of effectiveness which the wartime Fair Employment Practice Committee attained shows that it is possible to equalize job opportunity by Government action and thus to eliminate the influence of prejudice in employment.

Interstate Transportation

The channels of interstate commerce should be open to all Americans on a basis of complete equality. The Supreme Court has recently declared unconstitutional State laws requiring segregation on public carriers in interstate travel. Company regulations must not be allowed to replace unconstitutional State laws. I urge the Congress to prohibit discrimination and segregation, in the use of interstate transportation facilities, by both public officers and the employees of private companies.

The District of Columbia

I am in full accord with the principle of local self-government for residents of the District of Columbia. In addition, I believe that the Constitution should be amended to extend suffrage in Presidential elections to the residents of the District.

The District of Columbia should be a true symbol of American freedom and democracy for our own people, and for the people of the world. It is my earnest hope that the Congress will promptly give the citizens of the District of Columbia their own local, elective government. They themselves can then deal with the inequalities arising from segregation in the schools and other public facilities, and from racial barriers to places of public accommodation which now exist for one-third of the District's population.

The present inequalities in essential services are primarily a problem for the District itself, but they are also of great concern to the whole Nation. Failing local corrective action in the near future, the Congress should enact a model civil-rights law for the Nation's Capital.

Our Territories and Possessions

The present political status of our Territories and possessions impairs the enjoyment of civil rights by their residents. I have in the past recommended legislation granting statehood to Alaska and Hawaii, and organic acts for Guam and American Samoa, including a grant of citizenship to the people of these Pacific islands. I repeat these recommendations.

Furthermore, the residents of the Virgin Islands should be granted an increasing measure of self-government, and the people of Puerto Rico should be allowed to choose their form of government and their ultimate status with respect to the United States.

Equality in Naturalization

All properly qualified legal residents of the United States should be allowed to become citizens without regard to race, color, religion, or national origin. The Congress has recently removed the bars which formerly prevented persons from China, India, and the Philippines from becoming naturalized citizens. I urge the Congress to remove the remaining racial or nationality barriers which stand in the way of citizenship for some residents of our country.

Evacuation Claims of the Japanese-Americans

During the last war more than 100,000 Japanese-Americans were evacuated from their homes in the Pacific States solely because of their racial origin. Many of these people suffered property and business losses as a result of this forced evacuation and through no fault of their own. The Congress has before it legislation establishing a procedure by which claims based upon these losses can be promptly considered and settled. I trust that favorable action on this legislation will soon be taken.

The legislation I have recommended for enactment by the Congress at the present session is a minimum program if the Federal Government is to fulfill its obligation of insuring the constitutional guaranties of individual liberties and of equal protection under the law.

Under the authority of existing law, the Executive branch is taking every possible action to improve the enforcement of the civil-rights statutes and to eliminate discrimination in Federal employment, in providing Federal services and facilities, and in the armed forces.

I have already referred to the establishment of the Civil Rights Division of the Department of Justice. The Federal Bureau of Investigation will work closely with this new Division in the investigation of Federal civil-rights cases. Specialized training is being given to the Bureau's agents so that they may render more effective service in this difficult field of law enforcement.

It is the settled policy of the United States Government that there shall be no discrimination in Federal employment or in providing Federal services and facilities. Steady progress has been made toward this objective in recent years. I shall shortly issue an Executive order containing a comprehensive restatement of the Federal nondiscrimination policy, together with appropriate measures to insure compliance.

During the recent war and in the years since its close we have made much progress toward equality of opportunity in our armed services without regard to race, color, religion, or national origin. I have instructed the Secretary of Defense to take steps to have the remaining instances of discrimination in the armed services eliminated as rapidly as possible. The personnel policies and practices of all the services in this regard will be made consistent.

I have instructed the Secretary of the Army to investigate the status of civil-rights in the Panama Canal Zone with a view to eliminating such discrimination as may exist there. If legislation is necessary, I shall make appropriate recommendations to the Congress.

The position of the United States in the world today makes it especially urgent that we adopt these measures to secure for all our people their essential rights.

The peoples of the world are faced with the choice of freedom or enslavement, a choice between a form of government which harnesses the state in the service of the individual and a form of government which chains the individual to the needs of the state.

We in the United States are working in company with other nations who share our desire for enduring world peace and who believe with us that, above all else, men must be free. We are striving to build a world family of nations—a world where men may live under governments of their own choosing and under laws of their own making.

As part of that endeavor, the Commission on Human Rights of the United Nations is now engaged in preparing an international bill of human rights by which the nations of the world may bind themselves by international covenant to give effect to basic human rights and fundamental freedoms. We have played a leading role in this undertaking designed to create a world order of law and justice fully protective of the rights and the dignity of the individual.

To be effective in these efforts, we must protect our civil rights so that by providing all our people with the maximum enjoyment of personal freedom and personal opportunity we shall be a stronger nation—stronger in our leadership, stronger in our moral position, stronger in the deeper satisfactions of a united citizenry.

We know that our democracy is not perfect. But we do know that it offers a fuller, freer, happier life to our people than any totalitarian nation has ever offered.

If we wish to inspire the peoples of the world whose freedom is in jeopardy, if we wish to restore hope to those who have already lost their civil liberties, if we wish to fulfill the promise that is ours, we must correct the remaining imperfections in our practice of democracy.

We know the way. We need only the will.

CHAPTER III

Fair Deal for the Negro

An address delivered by President Harry S. Truman on Commencement Day, June 16, 1952, Howard University, Washington, D. C. (From the *Congressional Record*, Eighty-second Congress, Second session. LXXXXVIII, pt. 10, pp. A3711-A3712.)

I am happy to be here at this Howard University commencement.

Dr. Johnson has asked me to come to your commencement several times and I am glad that I was able to do it before the end of my term in office.

You who are graduating here today can always be proud of this university. This institution was founded in 1867 to give meaning to the principles of freedom, and to make them work.

The founders of this university had a great vision. They knew that the slaves who had been set free needed a center of learning and higher education. They could foresee that many of the freedmen, if they were given the chance, would take their places among the most gifted and honored American citizens. And that is what has happened. The long list of distinguished Howard alumni proves that the vision of those who established this university was profoundly true.

This university has been a true institution of higher learning which has helped to enrich American life with the talents of a gifted people.

For example, every soldier and every civilian who receives the life-saving gift of a transfusion from a blood bank can be grateful to this university. For it was the work of a distinguished Howard University professor, the late Dr. Charles Drew, that made possible the very first blood bank in the whole world.

This is a practical illustration of the fact that talent and genius have no boundaries of race, or nationality, or creed. The United States needs the imagination, the energy and the skills of every one of our citizens.

Howard University has recognized this from the beginning. It has accepted among its students, faculty, and trustees, representatives of every race, every creed, and every nationality.

I wish I could say to you who are graduating today that no opportunity to use your skills and knowledge would ever be denied you. I can say this: I know what it means not to have opportunity. I wasn't able to go to college at all. I had to stay at home and work my family's farm.

Without Discrimination

You have been able to get the college education that is so important to everyone in this country. Some of us are denied opportunity for economic reasons. Others are denied opportunity because of racial prejudice and discrimination. I want to see things worked out so that everyone who is capable of it receives a good education. And I want to see everyone have a chance to put his education to good use, without unfair discrimination.

Our country is founded on the proposition that all men are created equal. This means that they should be equal before the law. They should enjoy equal political rights, and they should have equal opportunities for education, employment, and decent living conditions.

This is our belief, and we know it is right. We know it is morally right. And we have proved by experience that the more we practice that belief, the stronger, more vigorous, and happier our Nation becomes.

That is why 6 years ago I created the President's Committee on Civil Rights. Nearly 5 years have passed since this committee made its report to me and to the whole American people. Today I want to talk about some of the progress that has been made in those 5 years.

Back in 1947 a good many people advised me not to raise this whole question of civil rights. They said it would only make things worse. But you can't cure a moral problem or a social problem by ignoring it.

It is no service to the country to turn away from the hard problems—to ignore injustices and human suffering. It is simply not the American way of doing things. Of course, there are always a lot of people whose motto is "Don't rock the boat." They are so afraid of rocking the boat that they stop rowing. We can never get ahead that way.

If something is wrong, the thing to do is to dig it out, find out why it is wrong, and take sensible steps to put it right. We are all

Americans together, and we can solve our hard problems together, including the problem of race relations.

The experience of the last 5 years demonstrates clearly that this is true. Instead of making things worse, our efforts in the field of civil rights have made things better—better in all aspects of our national life and in all parts of our country. One of my southern friends said the other day, "The last 5 years are the best years in race relations this country has ever had." And the record proves it.

Of course, the forward movement did not begin with the civil-rights report. It was already in motion. It had been started in the nineteen thirties and had gained momentum during World War II.

Postwar Problem Cited

It looked for a while in 1946 and 1947 as if this progress would come to an end. You remember that, after the First World War, a wave of hate and violence and Ku Kluxism swept over the country. The problem we faced after the Second World War was this: Would we have to go through another experience such as that, or could we hold fast to the gains that had been made?

We did neither. Instead, we went forward. In many lines, we have made gains for human freedom and equality of opportunity that go far beyond anything accomplished during the war. And most of these gains have been permanent. They have been written quietly, but firmly, into our basic laws and our institutions. They will never be undone.

These things have been accomplished without dividing our people. None of the talk about the country being torn apart has come to pass. These things were done because people wanted them to be done. There has been a great working of the American conscience. All over the land there has been a growing recognition that injustice must go, and that the way of equal opportunity is better for all of us.

The civil rights report and the civil rights program give voice and expression to this great change of sentiment. They are the necessary instrument of progress. They are the trumpet blast outside the walls of Jericho—the crumbling walls of prejudice.

And their work is not yet done. We still have a long way to go.

I should like to turn to the record now, and speak of the progress that has been made, and the tasks that still await us.

First, in the field of political rights. In the last 5 years, two more States, Tennessee and South Carolina, have abolished the poll tax. Now there are only 5 poll tax States, where there were 11, not long ago.

Opportunities for all our citizens to participate in our political life have increased steadily and rapidly. Court decisions have given protection to the right of equal participation in primary elections.

These are notable advances. But there is still a lot to do. The poll tax and other discriminatory restrictions on voting should be removed in all the States.

Second, let's take the field of education. I am glad to say that the principle of no discrimination—the principle that has always been followed here at Howard University—is the law of this country today in institutions of higher learning supported by public funds.

Since the court decisions outlawing discrimination, more than a thousand Negro graduate and professional students have been accepted by 10 State universities that were closed to Negroes before. In the last 5 years, legislation has been passed in 10 other States to abolish segregation or discrimination in schools and colleges.

Prophecies Held Unfulfilled

And the gloomy prophecies of the opponents of civil rights have not been fulfilled. The universities have not been deserted. On the contrary, the faculties and students of the universities which are now open to all have welcomed and accepted the new students on their merits as individuals.

This is only one instance of the way educational opportunities have been opening up to Negroes in recent years. Since 1930, the enrollment of Negro college students has gone up eight times. Just stop and think what that means. For every 100 Negro college students enrolled in 1930 there are 800 today.

In the field of housing, we have also been making progress. The congested, segregated areas in our great cities are breeding grounds of poverty, delinquency, and poor health. We have been trying to improve conditions in these areas. A major step was taken in this direction when the Supreme Court outlawed the enforcement of restrictive covenants, which so often make bad housing conditions worse.

We have begun to make progress in public housing also. In 1950, 177 local public housing projects were freely opened to families of all races and creeds. This is an eight-fold increase in 8 years. And in the last few years, nine States and eight cities have forbidden discrimination or segregation in public housing.

Another problem is that of protecting the right to safety and security of the person. There is no more important duty of government.

We must protect our citizens from mob violence. And here again we have been moving forward.

In the last 5 years, two States have enacted anti-lynching laws, and four States and six cities have passed laws against wearing masks in public. The civil rights section of the Department of Justice and the FBI have used their powers to reinforce the State and local law enforcement agencies.

The latest instance was in Illinois, where the State governer stopped an outbreak of mob violence and the Federal authorities brought to justice the local law enforcement officers who abetted the mob.

This kind of action hasn't interfered with States' rights or upset our system of government. Most of our citizens, wherever they live, have welcomed it. They want to be helped in supressing lynching. And they would be helped by Federal legislation to safeguard the rights of individuals when local law enforcement officers fail in their duty. Such legislation ought to be on the books.

Anti-Bias Board Set Up

Now I would like to speak of something that gives me considerable pride. That is the progress in fair employment in Federal service.

If there is any place where fair employment practices ought to prevail, it is the Federal Government. But experience shows that the departments and agencies of the Federal Government, no less than other organizations, need to be helped and encouraged. Sometimes they need to be compelled. In 1948, I set up a fair employment board in the Civil Service Commission. This board has gone about its task quietly and effectively, and has done a great deal to insure the success of our nondiscrimination policy.

The Federal Government makes billions of dollars worth of contracts every year to buy the things it needs. The money to pay for these contracts comes from all the people, without discrimination. It should be spent in the same way—without discrimination. For over 10 years we have had a policy that every Government contract must contain a clause binding the contractor and his sub-contractors to practice nondiscrimination.

But it is not always easy to be sure that such a clause is being followed in practice. To meet that situation, I set up a committee on Government contract compliance last year. It is the duty of that committee to work with the contracting agencies and to help them get better compliance with the rule of nondiscrimination.

States and cities have also been going ahead to see that fair
employment practices are followed in their jurisdictions. In the last few
years, 11 States and 20 municipalities have adopted fair-employment
laws. Unions and employers in many places have voluntarily done away
with the color bar. And the results have been peaceful and beneficial.
None of the disorder that was so freely predicted has taken place.

Some of the greatest progress of all has been made in the armed
services. Service in the Armed Forces of our country is both a duty
and a right of citizenship. Every man or woman who enters one of our
services is certainly entitled to equal treatment and equal opportunity.

There has been a great deal of talk about the need for segregation
in the armed services. Some of our greatest generals have said that
our forces had to have segregated units. But our experience has proved
that this was nonsense.

Quite some time ago, the Navy and the Air Force eliminated all
racial distinctions, and the Army has been moving step by step toward
this goal. For over 2 years, every soldier coming into a training unit
has been assigned on a basis of individual merit without racial distinction.

In the Far East, when General Ridgway took command, he ordered
the progressive integration of all the troops in his command, and you
have seen the results in the wonderful performance of our troops in
Korea. Only recently, a similar order was issued by the European
command at the direction of the Secretary of the Army. From Tokyo
and Heidelberg these orders have gone out that will make our fighting
forces a more perfect instrument of democratic defense.

All these matters have been taken care of in a quiet and orderly
way. The prophets of doom have been proved wrong. The civil rights
program has not weakened our country—it has made our country
stronger. It has not made us less united—it has made us more united.

Much Remains to be Done

The progress we have made so far is a source of deep satisfaction
to all of us. But that does not mean we have reached the goal or
that we can stop working. Much remains to be done.

Voluntary action can carry us a long way, and we must encourage
it. State and local legislation is a necessity, and we must have it.

But let us remember this: The President's Committee on Civil
Rights led the way. The debate over the civil-rights program has
stimulated much of the progress of the last 5 years. We still need the
legislation I recommended to the Congress in 1948. Only two of the

recommendations I made in my civil-rights program have been adopted so far. I shall continue, in office or out, to urge the Congress to adopt the remainder.

I am not one of those who feel that we can leave these matters up to the State alone or that we can rely solely on the efforts of men of good will. Our Federal Government must live up to the ideals professed in our Declaration of Independence and the duties imposed upon it by our Constitution. The full force and power of the Federal Government must stand behind the protection of rights guaranteed by our Federal Constitution.

In this country of ours that we all love so much, we have built a way of life that has brought more satisfaction to more people than any other that has ever been devised. Our American way of life is the envy and the admiration of people everywhere in the world. But this fact should not make us proud and arrogant. It places a heavy—a critical responsibility upon us.

The technical skills and knowledge that have been brought to such perfection in our country depend upon scientific discoveries that have come to us from all over the world. We have used this knowledge to build for ourselves a prosperous and happy country, but we know that we hold these skills in trust for all mankind. It is not our way to use the power that has come to us to oppress or victimize others. Our way is to use the power that has come to us to lift up the weak and the downtrodden.

In many countries of the world, misery, poverty, and poor health are widespread. Some of these countries were formerly possessions or colonies. Their people are now determined to improve their welfare and to preserve national independence.

And we can help those new countries reach their goals.

Tells of Point Four Aid

One of the means to do this is our point four program, through which we are helping to bring better health, more education, more and better food to millions of people. Graduates of this university are working on point four teams in many countries throughout the world.

Negro professional workers from this and other universities are helping to cure sickness in Burma and Lebanon, to increase farm output in Liberia, to improve education in Ethiopia and Iran. They are working in India, and Thailand, and Indochina. In these and other countries,

Americans are working together, regardless of race, creed, or ancestry, to help the progress of mankind.

This American Nation of ours is great because of its diversity—because it is a people drawn from many lands and many cultures, bound together by the ideals of human brotherhood. We must remember these things as we go forward in our efforts for world peace.

We should realize that much of the trouble in the world today is the result of false ideas of racial superiority. In the past the conduct of the democratic nations has too often been marred by a racial pride that has left its scars on the relations between east and west.

Today, as we reach a fuller understanding of the brotherhood of man, we are laying aside these old prejudices. We are working with the new nations of Asia and Africa as equals. Anything less would be a betrayal of the democratic ideals we profess. Better than any other country, the United States can reach out, through our diversity of races and origins, and deal as man to man with the different peoples of the globe.

In this way—in this spirit—we can help other peoples to build better lives for themselves. We can show that free peoples working together can change misery to happiness.

There are those who have said that this is America's century, but we want it to be more than that. We want it to be humanity's century.

If all the people of the world, including the people of the Soviet Union, could know and appreciate this fact, lasting peace and universal justice would not be a dream. They would be a reality. With courage, with vision, and with God's help we will yet make these ideals a reality around the world.

CHAPTER IV

Against Communism; For the Constitution

An address delivered by President Harry S. Truman to the Federal
Bar Association, Washington, D. C., upon the occasion of the thirtieth
anniversary of its founding, April 24, 1950. (From the *New York Times*,
April 25, 1950, p. 4.)

Mr. President, distinguished guests, members of the Federal Bar
Association:

I am delighted to be at this dinner tonight, and to join in com-
memorating the thirtieth anniversary of the founding of this fine
organization of Federal lawyers.

You know, you have an unusual representation of the Government
here tonight. You have the Executive Branch of the Government
represented by the President and members of his Cabinet; you have
the Chief Justice and members of the greatest court on earth repre-
senting the Judicial branch of the Government and you have the
second most powerful man—sometimes I think he's the first most
powerful man—in the Government of the United States in the Speaker
of the House of Representatives, which represents the Legislative branch
of the Government.

It would be rather hard for me to deny that I am friendly to
lawyers. The record would speak against me if I should deny it.

Six of the nine members of my Cabinet are lawyers. So are quite
a few other top officials of the Executive Branch.

When you couple this with the fact that over half the House of
Representatives and about two-thirds of the Senate are lawyers, as
well as all of our Federal judges, of course, you can see that—so far
as the Government of the United States is concerned—the legal pro-
fession is not just a passing fancy. It's probably here to stay.

Our lawyers have a primary responsibility in the maintenance of justice. This is particularly true of the Government lawyers, whose first devotion must be to the public interest. The public interest does not mean only the interest of the Government. It means also the protection of the rights of individual citizens.

Our concept of justice represents a basic difference between our system of government and that of the totalitarian states. Justice is the foundation of true democracy. Our system of justice preserves the freedom and dignity of the individual, and his right to think and speak as he feels and to worship as he pleases. It protects him in the assertion of his rights even against his own government. It makes certain that his assertion of those rights will be fairly considered and justly decided.

But there is in the world today a tyrannical force which does not recognize justice as we know it. It's a force which crushes the minds and bodies of those under its control, and seeks to enlarge itself by aggression and by false promises of freedom and economic security.

Wherever this force extends, there is no freedom of speech, no freedom of religion, no freedom even of opinion. The State is the all-powerful arbiter of men's words and acts. Human dignity and human freedom are meaningless.

Against this tyrannical force, which we know as communism, the United States stands as the great champion of freedom. Against this force, the United States has developed and put into effect a positive program to strengthen freedom and real democracy. Our program is shaped to strengthen the United States and to help other free nations protect themselves against aggression and subversion.

Since the end of the war we've taken far-seeing steps, unprecedented in the history of the world, to help other free nations rebuild from the destruction of war and strengthen their democratic institutions. Our programs of foreign aid have made it possible for these free nations to resist Communist aggression.

The Greek-Turkish Aid Program, the Marshall Plan, the North Atlantic Treaty, the Military Assistance Program and our support of the United Nations are the major elements in our central policy to work for a peaceful and a prosperous world. We've taken the leadership in aiding underdeveloped areas, and in reducing trade barriers between nations. We're keeping our military forces strong and alert, and we are giving meaning and strength to our joint defense arrangements with other countries.

We've done all this because it represents enlightened self-interest. We know that the greatest threat to us does not come from the Communists in this country, where they are a noisy but a small and universally despised group. The greatest threat comes from Communist imperialism abroad, where the center of its military and economic strength lies. The real danger is that communism might overrun other free nations and thus strengthen itself for an ultimate attack upon us.

But although communism is not a major force in this country, we're taking no chances on its becoming a strong force. On the one hand, we are working to create conditions in the United States in which communism cannot possibly thrive. On the other hand, we're striking hard blows at communist subversion wherever it's found.

We're vigorously pressing domestic programs to improve the standard of living of our people, to assure equal opportunity for all, to promote their health and education, and their security and freedom. These programs were not specifically designed as anti-Communist measures. We would have had them even if there were not a single Communist in the world. Nevertheless, they are among the strongest anti-Communist weapons in our whole arsenal.

Communism has little appeal for people who are healthy, well-educated, prosperous and free. Moreover, there are few things that will do more to prevent the Communists from winning followers in other lands than a demonstration by the United States that democracy truly means a better, freer life for everybody.

While we've been working to improve our democracy, we've been fully aware of the threat of Communist subversion within our own borders. Through the Federal Bureau of Investigation and other security forces, through prosecutions in the courts by the Department of Justice, through our Federal Employee Loyalty Program, and in many other ways, we have vigorously attacked Communists wherever their activities become a threat to our liberty.

There's been so much confusion recently about who's doing what to defeat communism in this country, that I think the record should be set straight.

This Administration has fought Communism with action and not just with words. We've carried on this fight with every law on the statute books, and we've recommended new laws when we found they were necessary and could be framed without impairing the very freedoms we are seeking to protect.

No known instance of Communist subversion—or any other kind of subversion—has gone uninvestigated.

No case where the facts warranted has gone unprosecuted.

We have prosecuted and obtained convictions of eleven top-ranking members of the Communist party in this country. We have successfully prosecuted many other persons for crimes related to communism. We have also prosecuted and obtained conviction of a large number of alleged Communists on charge of contempt for refusing to testify before Federal grand juries or Congressional committees.

And these prosecutions have been carried on by the Attorney General's office in the Executive part of the Government.

We now have under investigation the cases of over 1,000 citizens to determine whether steps should be taken to revoke their citizenship on grounds involving subversive activities. One hundred and thirty-eight persons are under orders of deportation on grounds involving communism.

There is no area of American life in which the Communist party is making headway, except, maybe, in the deluded minds of some people. The Communists have done their best to penetrate labor unions and the Government, but they are being successfully fought on both fronts. Labor has been doing a splendid job of cleaning its house. In the Federal Government, the employee loyalty program has been an outstanding success, and your Government lawyers have contributed greatly to its results.

I set up the employee loyalty program three years ago with two objectives in mind.

I was determined, as far as it was humanly possible, to see that no disloyal person should be employed by our Government, whether he was a Communist or a native American Fascist of the Silver Shirt or Ku Klux Klan variety. I was equally determined that loyal Government employees should be protected against accusations which were false, malicious and ill-founded. And that's as important as the other part of the program.

The loyalty program was drafted by able and experienced persons to protect the security of the Government and to safeguard the rights of its employees. It is the first time in the history of this country that we have had such a program. The Communists and their friends, as well as some sincere idealists, say that it is too drastic. The false patriots and even some honest reactionaries say that it is entirely too mild. They want us to dismiss employees on the basis of unsupported charges. They actually resent the Democratic safeguards of the loyalty program. All this confirms me in the conviction that it is a sound and effective program conceived and carried out in the American tradition. And that's just what it is.

The FBI, the agency loyalty boards, the Loyalty Review Board have quietly and effectively carried out their job of protecting the integrity and security of the Government of the United States. The Loyalty Review Board is the central organization which directs the whole program. It is divided about half and half between Democrats and Republicans and is headed by a distinguished Republican lawyer, Mr. Seth Richardson, who served as Assistant Attorney General of the United States under President Hoover.

Under the supervision of this board, the loyalty program has rid the Government of all employees who were found to be disloyal— and they were only a tiny fraction of 1 per cent.

Not a single person who has been adjudged to be a Communist or otherwise disloyal remains on the Government payroll today.

The able men charged with carrying out the loyalty program know that keeping disloyal persons out of the Government is a business which must be done carefully and objectively. They know that the job cannot be done by publicly denouncing men as "Communists" without having evidence to support such a charge, or by blackening the character of persons because their views are different from those of the accuser, or by hurling sensational accusations based on gossip, hearsay, or maybe just a hunch. They know that no one whose principal concern was the security of this country would try to do it that way. They know that anyone who had information about Communist activity or who placed the security of this country above selfish or partisan considerations would turn that information over to the FBI, so that it could be properly investigated and the necessary action taken.

I've been surprised to see how much ignorance and misunderstanding there is about this loyalty program—even on the part of persons who should know better. It has occurred to me that, perhaps, they do know better—or perhaps there is some element of politics in their accusations. Of course that couldn't be the case.

A large part of the hue and cry about the loyalty program has centered on my refusal to turn over to a Congressional committee confidential loyalty files concerning individual employees. I've already stated several times the reasons why these files must not be disclosed. I want to restate them briefly, now.

The preservation of the strictest confidence with respect to loyalty files is the single most important element in operating a loyalty program which provides effective security for the Government and justice for the individual employee.

The disclosures of these files would not only destroy the whole loyalty program but it would seriously damage the future usefulness of the FBI. Information is given to the FBI in confidence, which the FBI has sworn to protect. Breaking the confidence would not only greatly embarrass and even endanger the informants involved but would gravely impair the FBI's ability to get future information from other confidential sources.

Opening these files would reveal FBI procedures and methods. It might reveal highly secret information vital to our national security and of great value to foreign nations.

Disclosure of the files would result in serious injustice to the reputation of many innocent persons. This is true because the FBI investigative files do not contain proved information only. They include unverified charges and statements, as well as mere suspicions, which, upon investigation, are found to be untrue.

If I should now open these files, I would create a precedent for future cases in which access to these files is demanded—and there would be many of those requirements. This would completely destroy the loyalty program, since as experience shows, it would mean an attempt to try all loyalty cases over again in newspaper headlines, although they had already been carefully considered and fairly decided by a bi-partisan board of loyal and distinguished Americans.

This question of maintaining the confidential character of information which the President determines it would not be in the public interest to disclose is not new. It goes back to the beginning of our Government.

It started with Washington, was upheld by Monroe and Jackson and Grover Cleveland and Theodore Roosevelt and Franklin Roosevelt and half a dozen other Presidents I could name to you who have taken the same position which I am taking.

Nothing new at all. All you need to do is read your history and study the situation and you will find out that I'm right on it.

Despite the historic precedents, with which I was thoroughly familiar, I gave the most careful consideration to the recent request of the Senate committee for access to the loyalty files. I obtained the views of Attorney General McGrath, the Loyalty Review Board chairman Seth Richardson, and the FBI director Edgar Hoover before I reached my decision to deny this request. All three were unanimous in recommending to me in the strongest possible terms that I refuse to make the files available. The decision was mine to make, and I made it. I am confident that no President, whatever his party, would have acted otherwise. I'd do it again if necessary.

Now the Federal employee loyalty program has demonstrated that the United States has the most loyal civil service in the world. It's a splendid organization, and I'm proud to head it.

Of course, in an organization as large as the United States Government it is always possible, despite the greatest precautions, that there may be a few bad individuals. We shall not for one minute relax our vigilant efforts to protect the security of the Government of the United States. That's what I have sworn to do and that's what I intend to proceed to do to the best of my ability.

The present Attorney General and his predecessor have repeatedly asked that if any person has any information about the presence of any Communist in the Government, that it be furnished to them.

I now repeat that request.

That if there was anybody in the country who has any information that he feels would contribute to the safety and the welfare of the Government, all he has to do is to put it through the regular channels and if results are to be obtained they will be obtained. That's the only way you can do it, too.

If any citizen knows of the presence of a single Communist or other subversive person in any Federal job, let him furnish that information, and the evidence which supports his belief, to the Attorney General or to the FBI. Any information that may be furnished in response to this request will be promptly investigated and will be acted upon if the allegations are found to be true.

The fact of the matter is—because of the measures we are taking —the internal security of the United States is not seriously threatened by the Communists in this country. There are proportionately fewer Communists in this country than in any other large country on earth. They are noisy and they're troublesome, but they are not a major threat.

Moreover, they have been steadily losing ground since their peak in 1932, at the depth of our greatest depression, when they polled the largest number of votes in their history in this country.

There is a right way and a wrong way to fight communism. This Administration is doing it the right way and the sensible way.

Our atack on communism is embodied in a positive, threefold program:

One, we are strengthening our own defenses and aiding free nations in other parts of the world so that we and they can effectively resist Communist aggression.

Two, we are working to improve our democracy so as to give further proof, both to our own citizens and to people in other parts of the world, that democracy is the best system of government that men have yet devised.

Three, we are working quietly but effectively, without headlines or hysteria, against Communist subversion in this country wherever it appears, and we are doing this within the framework of the democratic liberties we cherish.

That's the way this Administration is fighting communism. That's the way it's going to continue to fight communism.

Now I am going to tell you how we are not going to fight Communism. We are not going to transform our fine FBI into a gestapo secret police. That's what some people would like to do. We are not going to try to control what our people read and say and think. We are not going to turn the United States into a Right-Wing totalitarian country in order to deal with a Left-Wing totalitarian threat.

In short, we're not going to end democracy. We're going to keep the Bill of Rights on the books. We're going to keep those ancient, hard-earned liberties which you lawyers have done so much to preserve and protect.

If we all work together to maintain and strengthen our democratic ideals, communism will never be a serious threat to our American way of life. The example we set for free men everywhere will help to roll back the tide of Communist imperialism in other parts of the world.

Now, I have outlined for you my program against communism. This is the way I've worked against it.

This is the way I shall continue.

And now, I call on all fair-minded men and women to join me in this good fight.

CHAPTER V

Security With Liberty

A message to the Congress of the United States from President Harry S. Truman, August 8, 1950. (From the *Congressional Record*, Eighty-first Congress, Second session. LXXXXVI, pt. 9, pp. 12018-12020.)

To the Congress of the United States:

I am presenting to the Congress certain considerations concerning the steps we need to take to preserve our basic liberties and to protect the internal security of the United States in this period of increasing international difficulty and danger. We face today, as we have always faced in time of international tension, the question of how to keep our freedom secure against internal as well as external attack, without at the same time unduly limiting individual rights and liberties.

Throughout our history as a Nation, our people have always—and properly—been wary of Government action which limited personal liberty. At the time our Constitution was being debated, there was considerable fear that it did not properly safeguard the exercise of individual freedom. As a result, the first 10 amendments to the Constitution —the Bill of Rights—were adopted, in order to make sure that the Federal Government would not infringe upon the free exercise of religion, freedom of speech, freedom of the press, the right of peaceable assembly, and the other basic rights which are essential in a free society. The Bill of Rights was then, and remains today, a stirring embodiment of our democratic ideals—an inspiration to freemen everywhere and to those who would be free.

At the same time, the Bill of Rights was not intended to prevent the Government from maintaining our Nation's integrity against subversion or attack. For example, the right of the people to keep and bear arms, which is guaranteed in the Bill of Rights, obviously gives no license for the building up of an armed revolutionary movement within our borders.

Accordingly, the Government has enacted laws, from time to time, against espionage, sabotage, and other internal threats to our national safety. Each of these laws necessarily places some restrictions on individual liberty, for the protection of the Nation.

It has always been difficult to draw the line between restrictions which are proper because they are necessary for internal security, and restrictions which are improper because they violate the spirit of the letter of the Constitution. It is clear that on certain occasions, that line has been overstepped.

Soon after our Government began functioning under the Constitution, there was enacted, in 1798, the group of legislative acts known as the alien and sedition laws. These laws were ostensibly designed to prevent activities which would undermine the Nation's safety and independence. But in fact they were broad enough and were used to imprison many leading citizens, including a Member of Congress, who expressed disagreement with the policies of the administration then in office.

The alien and sedition laws were so repugnant to the free spirit of our people that they played an important part in the disappearance of the Federalist Party, which sponsored them, and the objectionable features of these laws were shortly repealed or allowed to expire. That experience taught us a great lesson: that extreme and arbitrary security measures strike at the very heart of our free society, and that we must be eternally vigilant against those who would undermine freedom in the name of security.

Since the time of the alien and sedition laws, there have been recurrent periods—especially in wartime—when the safety of our Nation has been in danger. Each of these occasions has confronted us with a new set of conditions, to which we have had to adjust our internal-security laws and procedures.

At the same time, each of these periods of danger has been seized on by those who, in good faith or bad, would severely limit the freedom of our people in a misguided attempt to gain greater security. As we look back now, we can see that there have been certain times when we have, to some extent, repudiated our own ideals of freedom in an excess of zeal for our safety. Nevertheless, it is a tribute to the strong faith and common sense of our people that we have never for long been misled by the hysterical cries of those who would suppress our constitutional freedoms.

The present period is one of the times in which it has been necessary to adjust our security measures to new circumstances. The particular danger which we have had to meet has been created by the rise of totalitarianism—first, the totalitarianism of the right, and now that of the left.

Today we face most acutely the threat of the Communist movement, international in scope, directed from a central source, and committed to the overthrow of democratic institutions throughout the world.

The major danger from the Communist movement lies in its use of armed force and the threat of aggression through which it is trying to establish its control over free nations. To meet this danger we are working vigorously with other free nations to build a strong and effective common defense.

Communist imperialism also seeks to weaken and overthrow free nations by working within their borders.

Through their own political parties, and by trying to make alliances with non-Communist political groups, the Communists attempt to gain political power. The best defense against this aspect of the Communist threat is a vigorous, functioning democracy which succeeds in meeting the needs of its people. A vigilant people, who exercise their democratic rights to keep their government active in the interests of all, can defeat the efforts of Communists to attain electoral power.

In the United States the Communist Party has never received more than a minute portion of the national vote. The good sense of the American people, and their faith in democracy, have utterly rejected the false political appeal of communism.

As a part of their campaign to weaken free nations from within, the Communists try to infiltrate and gain control of the most vital citizens' organizations, such as unions, associations of veterans, business groups, and charitable, educational, and political societies. In this country these attempts have—with few exceptions—been successfully thwarted by the common sense and hard work of the members of those organizations, who have defeated the Communists through democratic processes, or forced them into isolated groups which are clearly and definitely identified as Communist-controlled.

The success of our labor-union members and leaders in exposing and eliminating Communists who had managed to gain positions of authority in the labor movement is particularly noteworthy. This demonstrates that open and public democratic processes provide the most effective way to prevent Communists from dominating the activities and policies of private groups in our country.

If the Communists confined their activities in this country to the open and public channels of the democratic process we would have little concern about them. But they do not so limit their activities. Instead, to serve the ends of a foreign power, they engage in espionage, sabotage, and other acts subversive of our national safety.

To protect us against activities such as these we must rely primarily upon Government action. We must have effective internal-security measures to prevent acts which threaten our national safety.

These measures must be accurately devised to meet real dangers. They must not be so broad as to restrict our liberty unnecessarily, for that would defeat our own ends. Unwise or excessive security measures can strike at the freedom and dignity of the individual which are the very foundation of our society—and the defense of which is the whole purpose of our security measures.

In considering the laws that are needed to protect our internal security against Communist activities, we should remember that we already have tested legal defenses against treason, espionage, sabotage, and other acts looking toward the overthrow of our Government by force or violence. Strong laws exist on the statute books—a number of them enacted or strengthened in recent years—under which we have proceeded and are proceeding vigorously against such crimes.

The treason laws make it a crime for anyone owing allegiance to the United States to levy war against his country, to give aid and comfort to its enemies, or to conceal knowledge concerning treasonable activities.

The espionage laws make it a crime to gather, give, receive, or transmit documents or similar materials concerning the national defense of the United States with intent or reason to believe that they are to be used against the interest of the United States. Furthermore, these laws make it a crime for anyone who has national defense information to communicate it to any person not entitled to receive it.

The sabotage laws make it a crime for anyone, with intent to interfere with the national defense, to attempt to injure or destroy any material, premises, or utilities which are important to the national defense.

There are other laws which make it a crime for two or more persons to "conspire to overthrow, put down, or to destroy by force the Government of the United States * * * or by force to prevent, hinder, or delay the execution of any law of the United States." There are also laws which make it a crime to advocate or teach the overthrow of the United States Government, or any State or local government, by force or violence, to organize any group for that purpose, or to be a member of such a group knowing its purpose. In 1948, 11 of the most important leaders of the Communist Party in this country were indicted under these laws. After a long trial, all were convicted, and their conviction was affirmed by an appellate court on August 1, 1950.

In addition to the criminal laws outlined above, there is a set of laws governing immigration, naturalization, and travel between our country and others. These laws permit the Government to exclude or deport any alien from this country who may be dangerous to our internal security, and to forbid or to regulate the travel abroad of United States citizens who may be engaged in subversive activity.

The laws I have been describing apply to private citizens and groups. A special set of laws and procedures applies to Government employees. Here our purpose is to exclude or remove from Government service persons who may be disloyal, even though they have committed no crime, and to keep from positions of importance persons who cannot be trusted to maintain security regulations, even though they may be loyal citizens and satisfactory employees in all other respects.

More than 3 years ago, the executive branch revised and improved its procedures for dealing with questions of employee loyalty and security. These new procedures have proved effective in protecting the Government against disloyal persons and persons whose employment constitutes a security risk.

The various laws and procedures I have outlined make up a strong set of legal safeguards against acts by individuals and groups which strike at the internal security of the United States.

Over the last few years, we have successfully prosecuted several hundred cases in the courts under existing internal security laws. In this process we have obtained a great deal of experience in the application of these laws. We have discovered a few defects, some of them minor and others of greater importance, in some of the existing statutes. In view of the situation which confronts us, it is important that these defects be remedied. At this time, therefore, I wish to recommend that the Congress enact certain legislation before the close of the present session.

First, I recommend that the Congress remedy certain defects in the present laws concerning espionage, the registration of foreign agents, and the security of national defense installations, by clarifying and making more definite certain language in the espionage laws, by providing an extended statute of limitations (in place of the present 3-year statute) for peacetime espionage, by requiring persons who have received instruction from a foreign government or political party in espionage or subversive tactics to register under the Foreign Agents Registration Act, and by giving broader authority than now exists for the President to establish security regulations concerning the protection of military bases and other national defense installations.

Second, I recommend that the Congress enact legislation permitting the Attorney General to exercise supervision over aliens subject to deportation and to require them, under the sanction of criminal penalties, to report their whereabouts and activities at regular intervals. In a number of cases, aliens under deportation orders cannot be deported because no other country will accept them. A bill pending before the Congress would permit the Attorney General in certain cases to detain such aliens in his custody for indefinite periods of time—not pursuant to a conviction for crime but on the basis of an administrative determination. Such action would be repugnant to our traditions, and it should not be authorized. Present law, however, is inadequate to permit proper supervision of deportable aliens, and should be strengthened as I have indicated.

Under the leadership of the National Security Council, the agencies of the Government which administer our internal security laws are keeping these laws under constant study to determine whether further changes are required to provide adequate protection. If it does appear that further improvements in these laws are needed, I shall recommend them to the Congress.

By building upon the framework now provided by our basic laws against subversive activities, we can provide effective protection against acts which threaten violence to our Government or to our institutions, and we can do this without violating the fundamental principles of our Constitution.

Nevertheless, there are some people who wish us to enact laws which would seriously damage the right of free speech and which could be used not only against subversive groups but against other groups engaged in political or other activities which were not generally popular. Such measures would not only infringe on the Bill of Rights and the basic liberties of our people; they would also undermine the very internal security they seek to protect.

Laws forbidding dissent do not prevent subversive activities; they merely drive them into more secret and more dangerous channels. Police states are not secure; their history is marked by successive purges, and growing concentration camps, as their governments strike out blindly in fear of violent revolt. Once a government is committed to the principle of silencing the voice of opposition, it has only one way to go, and that is down the path of increasingly repressive measures, until it becomes a source of terror to all its citizens and creates a country where everyone lives in fear.

We must, therefore, be on our guard against extremists who urge us to adopt police state measures. Such persons advocate breaking down the guaranties of the Bill of Rights in order to get at the Communists. They forget that if the Bill of Rights were to be broken down, all groups, even the most conservative, would be in danger from the arbitrary power of government.

Legislation is now pending before the Congress which is so broad and vague in its terms as to endanger the freedoms of speech, press, and assembly protected by the first amendment. Some of the proposed measures would, in effect, impose severe penalties for normal political activities on the part of certain groups, including Communists and Communist Party-line followers. This kind of legislation is unnecessary, ineffective, and dangerous.

It is unnecessary because groups such as the Communists cannot accomplish their evil purposes in this country through normal political activity. They will be repudiated by the people as they have always been.

It is ineffective because it does not get at the real dangers from the Communists in this country. These dangers come, not from normal political activity, but from espionage, sabotage, and the building up of an organization dedicated to the destruction of our Government by violent means—against all of which we already have laws.

This kind of proposed legislation is dangerous because, in attempting to proscribe, for groups such as the Communists, certain activities that are perfectly proper for everyone else, such legislation would spread a legal dragnet sufficiently broad to permit the prosecution of people who are entirely innocent or merely misguided. As far as the real conspirators against our institutions are concerned, such legislation would merely have the effect of driving them further underground and making it more difficult to reach them. Furthermore, if such legislation were held unconstitutional, as it well might be, it would make martyrs out of our worst enemies and create public sympathy for them.

Extreme proposals of this type reflect the widespread public concern about communism which most of our people feel today. In some communities, this concern has resulted in the enactment of unnecessary or unconstitutional laws or ordinances designed to suppress subversive activity.

We must not be swept away by a wave of hysteria.

It is natural, perhaps, to think that we can wipe out the dangers which confront us by passing a law. But we cannot get rid of communism just by passing a law. We must, of course, have effective legal defenses, but the principal protection of a free society against subversion is an alert and responsible citizenry dedicated to the advancement of freedom through democratic means.

This is the way to build real security for our country—and every citizen can help. Everyone in public life has a responsibility to conduct himself so as to reinforce and not undermine our internal security and our basic freedoms. Our press and radio have the same responsibility. Private groups of all kinds and citizens in their daily work and in their homes are equally concerned with the question of protecting our liberties and our national security. We must all act soberly and carefully, in keeping with our great traditions. This is important not only to our own country but to the success of the cause of freedom in the world.

Throughout the world, communism is seeking to discredit our system of constitutional liberties. The Communists know that the leadership and good will which our Nation enjoys arise in great measure from the fact that men here have the blessings of liberty. Consequently, the propaganda of communism is devoted to a bitter and unceasing attempt to blacken and distort our national character and our way of life.

This propaganda is a formidable threat to the unity of the free nations in working for peace. The best answer to it is not words, but deeds. We must demonstrate that we are a country in which men can live together and advance together as a free society. This alone can prove the falseness of the Communist attack. It would be tragic in the highest degree if we were to frighten ourselves into destroying those very liberties which are the basis of our moral leadership in the struggle for peace.

I am determined that the United States shall be secure. I am equally determined that we shall keep our historic liberties.

Success in achieving both these objectives is of exceptional importance in the present period of international tension. For by our actions we must maintain the United States as a strong, free people, confident in our liberties, and moving forward with other free peoples to oppose aggression and to build a just peace for all mankind.

CHAPTER VI

Veto of the Internal Security Act of 1950

A Message to the House of Representatives of the Congress of the United States from President Harry S. Truman, September 22, 1950. (From the *Congressional Record*, Eighty-first Congress, Second session. LXXXXVI, pt. 11, pp. 15629-15632.)

To the House of Representatives:

I return herewith, without my approval, H. R. 9490, the proposed "Internal Security Act of 1950."

I am taking this action only after the most serious study and reflection and after consultation with the security and intelligence agencies of the Government. The Department of Justice, the Department of Defense, the Central Intelligence Agency, and the Department of State have all advised me that the bill would seriously damage the security and intelligence operations for which they are responsible. They have strongly expressed the hope that the bill would not become law.

This is an omnibus bill containing many different legislative proposals with only one thing in common: they are all represented to be "anticommunist." But when the many complicated pieces of the bill are analyzed in detail, a startling result appears.

H. R. 9490 would not hurt the Communists. Instead, it would help them.

It has been claimed over and over again that this is an "anticommunist" bill—a "Communist control" bill. But in actual operation the bill would have results exactly the opposite of those intended.

It would actually weaken our existing internal security measures and would seriously hamper the Federal Bureau of Investigation and our other security agencies.

It would help the Communists in their efforts to create dissension and confusion within our borders.

It would help the Communist propagandists throughout the world who are trying to undermine freedom by discrediting as hypocrisy the efforts of the United States on behalf of freedom.

Specifically, some of the principal objections to the bill are as follows:

1. It would aid potential enemies by requiring the publication of a complete list of vital defense plants, laboratories, and other installations.

2. It would require the Department of Justice and its Federal Bureau of Investigation to waste immense amounts of time and energy attempting to carry out its unworkable registration provisions.

3. It would deprive us of the great assistance of many aliens in intelligence matters.

4. It would antagonize friendly governments.

5. It would put the Government of the United States in the thought-control business.

6. It would make it easier for subversive aliens to become naturalized as United States citizens.

7. It would give Government officials vast powers to harrass all of our citizens in the exercise of their right of free speech.

Legislation with these consequences is not necessary to meet the real dangers which communism presents to our free society. Those dangers are serious and must be met. But this bill would hinder us, not help us, in meeting them. Fortunately, we already have on the books strong laws which give us most of the protection we need from the real dangers of treason, espionage, sabotage, and actions looking to the overthrow of our Government by force and violence. Most of the provisions of this bill have no relation to these real dangers.

One provision alone of this bill is enough to demonstrate how far it misses the real target. Section 5 would require the Secretary of Defense to "proclaim" and "have published in the Federal Register" a public catalogue of defense plants, laboratories, and all other facilities vital to our national defense—no matter how secret. I cannot imagine any document a hostile foreign government would desire more. Spies and saboteurs would willingly spend years of effort seeking to find out the information that this bill would require the Government to hand them on a silver platter. There are many provisions of this bill which impel me to return it without my approval, but this one would be enough by itself. It is inconceivable to me that a majority of the Congress could expect the Commander in Chief of the Armed Forces of the United States to approve such a flagrant violation of proper security safeguards.

This is only one example of many provisions in the bill which would in actual practice work to the detriment of our national security.

I know that the Congress had no intention of achieving such results when it passed this bill. I know that the vast majority of the Members of Congress who voted for the bill sincerely intended to strike a blow at the Communists.

It is true that certain provisions of this bill would improve the laws protecting us against espionage and sabotage. But these provisions are greatly outweighed by others which would actually impair our security.

I repeat, the net results of this bill would be to help the Communists, not to hurt them.

I therefore most earnestly request the Congress to reconsider its action. I am confident that on more careful analysis most Members of Congress will recognize that this bill is contrary to the best interests of our country at this critical time.

H. R. 9490 is made up of a number of different parts. In summary, their purposes and probable effects may be described as follows:

Sections 1 through 17 are designed for two purposes. First, they are intended to force Communist organizations to register and to divulge certain information about themselves—information on their officers, their finances, and, in some cases, their membership. These provisions would in practice be ineffective, and would result in obtaining no information about Communists that the FBI and our other security agencies do not already have. But in trying to enforce these sections, we would have to spend a great deal of time, effort and money —all to no good purpose.

Second, these provisions are intended to impose various penalties on Communists and others covered by the terms of the bill. So far as Communists are concerned, all these penalties which can be practicably enforced are already in effect under existing laws and procedures. But the language of the bill is so broad and vague that it might well result in penalizing the legitimate activities of people who are not Communists at all, but loyal citizens.

Thus the net result of these sections of the bill would be: no serious damage to the Communists, much damage to the rest of us. Only the Communist movement would gain from such an outcome.

Sections 18 through 21 and section 23 of this bill constitute, in large measure, the improvements in our internal security laws which I recommended some time ago. Although the language of these sections is in some respects weaker than is desirable, I should be glad to approve these provisions if they were enacted separately, since they are improvements developed by the FBI and other Government security agencies to meet certain clear deficiencies of the present law. But even though these improvements are needed, other provisions of the bill would weaken our security far more than these would strengthen it. We have better protection for our internal security under existing law than we would have with the amendments and additions made by H. R. 9490.

Sections 22 and 25 of this bill would make sweeping changes in our laws governing the admission of aliens to the United States and their naturalization as citizens.

The ostensible purpose of these provisions is to prevent persons who would be dangerous to our national security from entering the country or becoming citizens. In fact, present law already achieves that objective.

What these provisions would actually do is to prevent us from admitting to our country, or to citizenship, many people who could make real contributions to our national strength. The bill would deprive our Government and our intelligence agencies of the valuable services of aliens in security operations. It would require us to exclude and to deport the citizens of some friendly non-Communist countries. Furthermore, it would actually make it easier for subversive aliens to become United States citizens. Only the Communist movement would gain from such actions.

Section 24 and sections 26 through 30 of this bill make a number of minor changes in the naturalization laws. None of them is of great significance—nor are they particularly relevant to the problem of internal security. These provisions, for the most part, have received little or no attention in the legislative process. I believe that several of them would not be approved by the Congress if they were considered on their merits, rather than as parts of an omnibus bill.

Section 31 of this bill makes it a crime to attempt to influence a judge or jury by public demonstration, such as picketing. While the courts already have considerable power to punish such actions under existing law, I have no objection to this section.

Sections 100 through 117 of this bill (title II) are intended to give the Government power, in the event of invasion, war, or insurrection in the United States in aid of a foreign enemy, to seize and hold persons who could be expected to attempt acts of espionage or sabotage, even though they have had as yet committed no crime. It may be that legislation of this type should be on the statute books. But the provisions in H. R. 9490 would very probably prove ineffective to achieve the objective sought, since they would not suspend the writ of habeas corpus, and under our legal system to detain a man not charged with a crime would raise serious constitutional questions unless the writ of habeas corpus were suspended. Furthermore, it may well be that other persons than those covered by these provisions would be more important to detain in the event of emergency. This whole problem, therefore, should clearly be studied more thoroughly before further legislative action along these lines is considered.

In brief, when all the provisions of H. R. 9490 are considered together, it is evident that the great bulk of them are not directed toward the real and present dangers that exist from communism. Instead of striking blows at communism, they would strike blows at our own liberties and at our position in the forefront of those working for freedom in the world. At a time when our young men are fighting for freedom in Korea, it would be tragic to advance the objectives of communism in this country, as this bill would do.

Because I feel so strongly that this legislation would be a terrible mistake, I want to discuss more fully its worse features—sections 1 through 17, and sections 22 and 25.

Most of the first 17 sections of H. R. 9490 are concerned with requiring registration and annual reports, by what the bill calls Communist-action organizations and Communist-front organizations, of names of officers, sources and uses of funds, and, in the case of Communist-action organizations, names of members.

The idea of requiring Communist organizations to divulge information about themselves is a simple and attractive one. But it is about as practical as requiring thieves to register with the sheriff. Obviously, no such organization as the Communist Party is likely to register voluntarily.

Under the provisions of the bill, if an organization which the Attorney General believes should register does not do so, he must request a five-man Subversive Activities Control Board to order the organization to register. The Attorney General would have to produce proof that the organization in question was in fact a Communist-action or a Communist-front organization. To do this he would have to offer evidence relating to every aspect of the organization's activities. The organization could present opposing evidence. Prolonged hearings would be required to allow both sides to present proof and to cross-examine opposing witnesses.

To estimate the duration of such a proceeding involving the Communist Party, we need only recall that on much narrower issues the trial of the 11 Communist leaders under the Smith Act consumed 9 months. In a hearing under this bill, the difficulties of proof would be much greater and would take a much longer time.

The bill lists a number of criteria for the Board to consider in deciding whether or not an organization is a Communist-action or Communist-front organization. Many of these deal with the attitudes or states of mind of the organization's leaders. It is frequently difficult in legal proceedings to establish whether or not a man has committed an overt act, such as theft or perjury. But under this bill, the Attorney General would have to attempt the immensely more difficult task of producing concrete legal evidence that men have particular ideas or opinions. This would inevitably require the disclosure of many of the FBI's confidential sources of information and thus would damage our national security.

If, eventually, the Attorney General should overcome these difficulties and get a favorable decision from the Board, the Board's decision could be appealed to the courts. The courts would review any questions of law involved, and whether the Board's findings of fact were supported by the preponderance of the evidence.

All these proceedings would require great effort and much time. It is almost certain that from 2 to 4 years would elapse between the Attorney General's decision to go before the Board with a case, and the final disposition of the matter by the courts.

And when all this time and effort had been spent, it is still most likely that no organization would actually register.

The simple fact is that when the courts at long last found that a particular organization was required to register, all the leaders of the organization would have to do to frustrate the law would be to dissolve the organization and establish a new one with a different name and a new roster of nominal officers. The Communist Party has done this again and again in countries throughout the world. And nothing could be done about it except to begin all over again the long dreary process of investigative, administrative, and judicial proceedings to require registration.

Thus the net result of the registration provision of this bill would probably be an endless chasing of one organization after another, with the Communists always able to frustrate the law enforcement agencies and prevent any final result from being achieved. It could only result in wasting the energies of the Department of Justice and in destroying the sources of information of its FBI. To impose these fruitless burdens upon the FBI would divert it from its vital security duties and thus give aid and comfort to the very Communists whom the bill is supposed to control.

Unfortunately, these provisions are not merely ineffective and unworkable. They represent a clear and present danger to our institutions.

Insofar as the bill would require registration by the Communist Party itself, it does not endanger our traditional liberties. However, the application of the registration requirements to so-called Communist-front organizations can be the greatest danger to freedom of speech, press and assembly, since the Alien and Sedition Laws of 1798. This danger arises out of the criteria or standards to be applied in determining whether an organization is a Communist-front organization.

There would be no serious problem if the bill required proof that an organization was controlled and financed by the Communist Party before it could be classified as a Communist-front organization. However, recognizing the difficulty of proving those matters, the bill would permit such a determination to be based solely upon the extent to which the positions taken or advanced by it from time to time on matters of policy do not deviate from those of the Communist movement.

This provision could easily be used to classify as a Communist-front organization any organization which is advocating a single policy or objective which is also being urged by the Communist Party or by a Communist foreign government. In fact, this may be the intended result, since the bill defines "organization" to include "a group of persons permanently or temporarily associated together for joint action on any subject or subjects." Thus, an organization which advocates low-cost housing for sincere humanitarian reasons might be classified as a Communist-front organization because the

Communist regularly exploit slum conditions as one of their fifth-column techniques.

It is not enough to say that this probably would not be done. The mere fact that it could be done shows clearly how the bill would open a Pandora's box of opportunities for official condemnation of organizations and individuals for perfectly honest opinions which happen to be stated also by Communists.

The basic error of these sections is that they move in the direction of suppressing opinion and belief. This would be a very dangerous course to take, not because we have any sympathy for Communist opinions, but because any governmental stifling of the free expression of opinion is a long step toward totalitarianism.

There is no more fundamental axiom of American freedom than the familiar statement: In a free country, we punish men for the crimes they commit, but never for the opinions they have. And the reason this is so fundamental to freedom is not, as many suppose, that it protects the few unorthodox from suppression by the majority. To permit freedom of expression is primarily for the benefit of the majority because it protects criticism, and criticism leads to progress.

We can and we will prevent espionage, sabotage, or other actions endangering our national security. But we would betray our finest traditions if we attempted, as this bill would attempt, to curb the simple expression of opinion. This we should never do, no matter how distasteful the opinion may be to the vast majority of our people. The course proposed by this bill would delight the Communists, for it would make a mockery of the Bill of Rights and of our claim to stand for freedom in the world.

And what kind of effect would these provisions have on the normal expression of political views? Obviously, if this law were on the statute books, the part of prudence would be to avoid saying anything that might be construed by someone as not deviating sufficiently from the current Communist propaganda line. And since no one could be sure in advance what views were safe to express, the inevitable tendency would be to express no views on controversial subjects.

The result could only be to reduce the vigor and strength of our political life—an outcome that the Communists would happily welcome, but that free men should abhor.

We need not fear the expression of ideas—we do need to fear their suppression.

Our position in the vanguard of freedom rests largely on our demonstration that the free expression of opinion, coupled with government by popular consent, leads to national strength and human advancement. Let us not, in cowering and foolish fear, throw away the ideals which are the fundamental basis of our free society.

Not only are the registration provisions of this bill unworkable and dangerous, they are also grossly misleading in that all but one of the objectives which are claimed for them are already being accomplished by other and superior methods—and the one objective which is not now being accomplished would not in fact be accomplished under this bill either.

It is claimed that the bill would provide information about the Communist Party and its members. The fact is, the FBI already possesses very complete sources of information concerning the Communist movement in this country. If the FBI must disclose its sources of information in public hearings to require registration under this bill, its present sources of information, and its ability to acquire new information, will be largely destroyed.

It is claimed that this bill would deny income-tax exemption to Communist organizations. The fact is that the Bureau of Internal Revenue already denies income-tax exemption to such organizations.

It is claimed that this bill would deny passports to Communists. The fact is that the Government can and does deny passports to Communists under existing law.

It is claimed that this bill would prohibit the employment of Communists by the Federal Government. The fact is that the employment of Communists by the Federal Government is already prohibited and, at least in the executive branch, there is an effective program to see that they are not employed.

It is claimed that this bill would prohibit the employment of Communists in defense plants. The fact is that it would be years before this bill would have any effect of this nature—if it ever would. Fortunately, this objective is already being substantially achieved under the present procedures of the Department of Defense, and if the Congress would enact one of the provisions I have recommended—which it did not include in this bill—the situation would be entirely taken care of, promptly and effectively.

It is also claimed—and this is the one new objective of the registration provisions of this bill—that it would require Communist organizations to label all their publications and radio and television broadcasts as emanating from a Communist source. The fact is that this requirement, even if constitutional, could be easily and permanently evaded, simply by the continuous creation of new organizations to distribute Communist information.

Section 4 (a) of the bill, like its registration provisions, would be ineffective, would be subject to dangerous abuse, and would seek to accomplish an objective which is already better accomplished under existing law.

This provision would make unlawful any agreement to perform any act which would substantially contribute to the establishment within the United States of a foreign-controlled dictatorship. Of course, this provision would be unconstitutional if it infringed upon the fundamental right of the American people to establish for themselves by constitutional methods any form of government they choose. To avoid this, it is provided that this section shall not apply to the proposal of a constitutional amendment. If this language limits the prohibition of the section to the use of unlawful methods, then it adds nothing to the Smith Act, under which 11 Communist leaders have been convicted, and would be more difficult to enforce. Thus, it would accomplish nothing. Moreover, the bill does not even purport to define the phrase, unique in a criminal statute, "substantially contribute." A phrase so vague raises a serious constitutional question.

Sections 22 and 25 of this bill are directed toward the specific questions of who should be admitted to our country, and who should be permitted to become a United States citizen. I believe there is general agreement that the answers to those questions should be: We should admit to our country, within the available quotas, anyone with a legitimate purpose who would not endanger our security, and we should admit to citizenship any immigrant who will be a loyal and constructive member of the community. Those are essentially the standards set by existing law. Under present law, we do not admit to our country known Communists, because we believe they work to overthrow our Government, and we do not admit Communists to citizenship, because we believe they are not loyal to the United States.

The changes which would be made in the present law by sections 22 and 25 would not reinforce those sensible standards. Instead, they would add a number of new standards, which, for no good and sufficient reason, would interfere with our relations with other countries and seriously damage our national security.

Section 22 would, for example, exclude from our country anyone who advocates any form of totalitarian or one-party government. We, of course, believe in the democratic system of competing political parties, offering a choice of candidates and policies. But a number of countries with which we maintain friendly relations have a different form of government.

Until now, no one has suggested that we should abandon cultural and commercial relations with a country merely because it has a form of government different from ours. Yet section 22 would require that. As one instance, it is clear that under the definitions of the bill the present Government of Spain, among others, would be classified as "totalitarian." As a result, the Attorney General would be required to exclude from the United States all Spanish businessmen, students, and other nonofficial travelers who support the present Government of their country. I cannot understand how the sponsors of this bill can think that such an action would contribute to our national security.

Moreover, the provisions of section 22 of this bill would strike a serious blow to our national security by taking away from the Government the power to grant asylum in this country to foreign diplomats who repudiate Communist imperialism and wish to escape its reprisals. It must be obvious to anyone that it is in our national interest to persuade people to renounce communism, and to encourage their defection from Communist forces. Many of these people are extremely valuable to our intelligence operations. Yet under this bill the Government would lose the limited authority it now has to offer asylum in our country as the great incentive for such defection.

In addition, the provisions of section 22 would sharply limit the authority of the Government to admit foreign diplomatic representatives and their families on official business. Under existing law, we already have the authority to send out of the country any person who abuses diplomatic privileges by working against the interests of the United States. But under this bill a whole series of unnecessary restrictions would be placed on the admission of diplomatic personnel. This is not only ungenerous, for a country which eagerly sought and proudly holds the honor of being the seat of the United Nations, it is also very unwise, because it makes our country appear to be fearful of foreigners, when in fact we are working as hard as we know how to build mutual confidence and friendly relations among the nations of the world.

Section 22 is so contrary to our national interests that it would actually put the Government into the business of thought control by requiring the deportation of any alien who distributes or publishes, or who is affiliated with an organization which distributes or publishes, any written or printed matter advocating (or merely expressing belief in) the economic and governmental doctrines of any form of totalitarianism.

This provision does not require an evil intent or purpose on the part of the alien, as does a similar provision in the Smith Act. Thus, the Attorney General would be required to deport any alien operating or connected with a well-stocked bookshop containing books on economics or politics written by supporters of the present government of Spain, of Yugoslavia or any one of a number of other countries. Section 25 would make the same aliens ineligible for citizenship. There should be no room in our laws for such hysterical provisions. The next logical step would be to "burn the books."

This illustrates the fundamental error of these immigration and naturalization provisions. It is easy to see that they are hasty and ill-considered. But far more significant—and far more dangerous— is their apparent underlying purpose. Instead of trying to encourage the free movement of people, subject only to the real requirements of national security, these provisions attempt to bar movement to anyone who is, or once was, associated with ideas we dislike, and in the process, they would succeed in barring many people whom it would be to our advantage to admit.

Such an action would be a serious blow to our work for world peace. We uphold—or have upheld till now, at any rate—the concept of freedom on an international scale. That is the root concept of our efforts to bring unity among the free nations and peace in the world.

The Communists, on the other hand, attempt to break down in every possible way the free interchange of persons and ideas. It will be to their advantage, and not ours, if we establish for ourselves an "iron curtain" against those who can help us in the fight for freedom.

Another provision of the bill which would greatly weaken our national security is section 25, which would make subversive aliens eligible for naturalization as soon as they withdraw from organizations required to register under this bill, whereas under existing law they must wait for a period of 10 years after such withdrawal before becoming eligible for citizenship. This proposal is clearly contrary to the national interest, and clearly gives to the Communists an advantage they do not have under existing law.

I have discussed the provisions of this bill at some length in order to explain why I am convinced that it would be harmful to our security and damaging to the individual rights of our people if it were enacted.

Earlier this month, we launched a great Crusade for Freedom designed, in the words of General Eisenhower, to fight the big lie with the big truth. I can think of no better way to make a mockery of that crusade and of the deep American belief in human freedom and dignity which underlie it than to put the provisions of H. R. 9490 on our statute books.

I do not undertake lightly the responsibility of differing with the majority in both Houses of Congress who have voted for this bill. We are all Americans; we all wish to safeguard and preserve our constitutional liberties against internal and external enemies. But I cannot approve this legislation, which instead of accomplishing its avowed purpose would actually interfere with our liberties and help the Communists against whom the bill was aimed.

This is a time when we must marshal all our resources and all the moral strength of our free system in self-defense against the threat of Communist aggression. We will fail in this, and we will destroy all that we seek to preserve, if we sacrifice the liberties of our citizens in a misguided attempt to achieve national security.

There is no reason why we should fail. Our country has been through dangerous times before, without losing our liberties to external attack or internal hysteria. Each of us, in Government and out, has a share in guarding our liberties. Each of us must search his own conscience to find whether he is doing all that can be done to preserve and strengthen them.

No considerations of expediency can justify the enactment of such a bill as this, a bill which would so greatly weaken our liberties and give aid and comfort to those who would destroy us. I have, therefore, no alternative but to return this bill without my approval, and I earnestly request the Congress to reconsider its action.

CHAPTER VII

Our Heritage of Freedom and Equality

An address delivered by President Harry S. Truman on Constitution Day, September 17, 1951, in the Library of Congress, Washington, D. C. (From the *Congressional Record*, Eighty-second Congress, First session. LXXXXVII, pt. 9, pp. 11542-11543.)

Mr. Chief Justice of the United States, Senator Green, Dr. Evans, distinguished guests, ladies, and gentlemen, we have met here this morning to put some pieces of parchment away in specially sealed cases, in order to preserve them from physical and chemical change.

And I can't help but be impressed with this magnificent collection of all the ancient, medieval, and modern documents that are in this Library. I think always of the terrible destruction of the Alexandrian Library in the Middle Ages. And this Library, the British Museum, and the Louvre are our modern replicas of that great Alexandrian Library. The documents which we are putting away today are written in a style of handwriting which is no longer familiar to us. If they were only historical relics, it might seem strange that we should make a ceremony out of this occasion of sealing them up.

But the Declaration of Independence and the Constitution are more than historical relics. They are a living force in our life today.

We may have some difficulty in preserving the parchment on which these two documents have been written, but the ideas they set forth will never perish. These documents express the highest principles of political life: That all men have certain inalienable rights, that governments are set up to provide for the welfare of the people, and that the rule of law stands above government and citizen alike.

These ideas have a life of their own. They have been a dynamic force in the history of our Nation. They have inspired men, all around the world, to create new and independent governments, and to improve the conditions under which they live.

Aimed Against Despotism

These are very explosive documents, Dr. Evans. We may think we have them safely bottled up, but the ideas they express will go on forever. They will continue to give energy and hope to new generations of men, here and in other countries, in the long struggle to create a better society on earth.

The Declaration of Independence and the Constitution, when they were written, were revolutionary documents. But they were revolutionary in a very unusual sense.

Many revolutions are simply a resort to force and violence to impose a new despotism upon the people. But these documents were for a very different purpose; their aim was to make despotism impossible. Both the Declaration of Independence and the Constitution seek to make the rule of law and the concepts of justice the dominating factors in government. And to a large extent they have succeeded.

The struggle against the use of naked force as an instrument of government was an old one even before these two documents were written. Our forefathers created a new nation, but they based it upon the long experience of the English people in maintaining human freedom.

Points to Basic Concepts

The right of trial by jury, the right to be free from unreasonable search and seizure, the right of habeas corpus, the prohibition against cruel and unusual punishment, the guaranties of freedom of the press, freedom of assembly, and freedom of religion—all these were basic concepts in the days of our revolution. They were concepts for which men had worked and even given up their lives for centuries.

But they had never been made the foundation stones of a government until they were put in the Declaration of Independence and in the Constitution and its first 10 amendments—the Bill of Rights—which are just as fundamental a part of our basic law as the original version of the Constitution that we are sealing up here today.

I hope that they will be sealed up and placed alongside the original document. In my opinion, they are the most important parts of the Constitution.

These rights have become so well established in this country that we take them for granted. They are so much a part of our lives that they may seem dry and uninteresting. But the history of other countries in recent years has showed us how vital and important they are. Recent history has demonstrated that the unrestrained use of force by government is just as great a danger to human progress now as it was ages ago. It has demonstrated that unless citizens have rights against the government no one can be safe or secure.

In our own lifetime we have learned anew the human misery that an absolute, power-mad government can create. We have seen it in the brief history of the Fascist and Nazi tyrannies. We are witnessing it today in the tyranny of Soviet communism.

A constitution is not just a matter of words. There are other constitutions which may read as well as ours.

Just take, for example, the constitution of the Soviet Union. That constitution has a lot of fine language and a lot of beautiful and meaningful words. That constitution of the Soviet Union says that Soviet citizens are guaranteed freedom of speech, freedom of press, and freedom of assembly. I wonder what would happen to a citizen of the Soviet Union if he tried to exercise any of those freedoms. It professes to guarantee that citizens of the Soviet Union shall be secure in their persons and their homes. And in addition, it purports to guarantee equality, the right to work, the right to an education, the right to rest and leisure, freedom of religion, and a lot of other fine things.

But these good words in the Soviet Constitution mean less than nothing. They are empty promises, because the citizens of the Soviet Union have no way of enforcing their rights against the state.

The constitutional guaranties are just as false as their treaty agreements. A Bolshevik agreement is not worth the paper it is written on. It is only a scrap of paper. I wonder what would happen to a citizen of the Soviet Union if he tried to exercise one of those freedoms.

In the Soviet Union, the power of the state is above all rights. The Government does not have to obey the law. As a result, the citizens of the Soviet Union enjoy none of the freedoms which they are guaranteed by their constitution. They do not have freedom of speech or freedom of the press. They may be arrested without cause; their homes may be invaded without a search warrant; they may be executed or exiled without a fair trial and without appeal.

Calls Soviet Society a Jungle

The Soviet citizens live in fear. Their society is a jungle, through which the naked power of the Government prowls like a beast of prey, making all men afraid.

The Communists claim that they have to use the weapons of tyranny in order to improve the conditions of the people. But that is not true. That is a rejection of the long experience of mankind. By resorting to the worst evils of ancient tyranny, the Soviet rulers have held their citizens in terror and bondage, while freedom is growing in the rest of the world.

And the evils which the Communists brought back into the world—the evils of political persecution and unrestrained state power—have grown and flourished, and become much more terrible than they ever were before. Modern inventions, modern means of communication, modern methods of propaganda make the power of the state more formidable than it was in the days of the stage coach and the muzzle-loading musket. The power of the Kremlin is more effective, more violent, more far-reaching than the power of the Czars or the power of Genghis Khan or the power of other tyrants of the past.

Today, the tyrant can uproot and liquidate whole classes of people and entire nations. The death camps of Hitler Germany or of modern Siberia demonstrate that the unrestrained power of the government can be a greater evil in our modern civilization than it ever was in ancient times.

Safeguards for Freedom Stressed

The only guaranty against such a society of fear and cruelty is the principle that the government is not above the law. Our Declaration of Independence and our Constitution proclaim that the Government is subject to the fundamental law.

The Constitution sets up a system of internal checks and balances which may seem cumbersome to us at times, but which succeeds in preventing any part of the Government from having absolute power. Under our Constitution, it is not only the citizens who are made to conform to the principles of justice but the Government itself. And the citizen has the power to enforce his rights against the Government. The rule of law is made supreme.

Our Constitution protects us from the evils of tyranny. But this is not all our Constitution does. If it were, it would not be enough.

A constitution must do more than provide restraints against the illegal use of power. It must give the people a means of dealing with their day-to-day problems, of continually correcting the injustices that spring up in human society. A constitution that is not adaptable—that prevents the government from acting for the general welfare of the people—will not long survive. It will become a mere historical curiosity.

Ours is not such a constitution. We have discovered over the years that it offers the means for correcting present evils without throwing away past gains.

Great Advances Are Listed

There are always those who oppose necessary reforms. Such people often turn to the Constitution to justify their position. But our Constitution has seldom proved to be a barrier to changes which were needed for the welfare of all the people. Our Constitution has not set up aristocracy of wealth or privilege. It does not serve the privileged few at the expense of the great majority of the people.

The great advances we have made in recent years in legislation to improve the condition of labor, to bring economic security to the farmer, to provide aid for the needy, to develop the resources of the country for the benefit of all, to improve health, the education, and the housing of the average family—all these advances have been opposed in the name of the Constitution. But it never was the purpose of the Constitution to bar such advances. On the contrary, the Constitution provides the means for carrying into effect the fundamental ideas of justice and liberty and human progress on which our Government is founded.

Acting under our Constitution, we have been able to solve the problems which have driven other countries into revolution. We have been able to make necessary reforms without overthrowing the ancient guaranties of our liberty. Building on the experience of the past we have opened the way to a brighter future.

Urges Documents Be Cherished

On this occasion, we ought to pray to Almighty God that the American people will remain faithful to the spirit of the Declaration of Independence and the Constitution. We should ask that they be ever mindful of the great wisdom and the truth that are embodied in these two documents, and through them, in our form of government.

The wisdom of our form of government is that no men, no matter how good they may appear to be, may be entrusted with absolute power. The great achievement of our form of government is that it has enabled us to meet the changing needs of the people while providing a rule of law that restrains all men, even the most powerful. The glory of our form of government lies in the fact that it has held us faithful to the concept that the aims of government are human betterment and human freedom.

If the American people remember these things and understand them well, this Nation will move forward in the future as it has in the past. And these documents, which we are today sealing against physical decay, will always be remembered and cherished, finding new life in each new generation of Americans.

CHAPTER VIII

What Hysteria Does to Us

An address delivered by the Honorable Harry S. Truman at Westminster College, Fulton, Missouri, on April 12, 1954, under the auspices of the John Findley Green Foundation. (From the mimeographed text released to the press at the time of the address, a copy of which is in the possession of Westminster College.)

A little over eight years ago it was my pleasure to introduce from this platform one of the world's great men, Winston Churchill.

I was President of the United States at that time. He was just a private citizen, if one can use the word private in association with the name of Winston Churchill.

Today there seems to be a slight change. I am the private citizen now. Churchill is again Prime Minister.

And if what I read in the newspapers is true, then I suppose Winston Churchill would be happier if he were here again today.

Of course, that dauntless British statesman is where he should be, giving his countrymen and the world untiring service and leadership.

I am particularly mindful, as I recall Churchill's appearance here, of the tradition and background of law which is the common basis of our two democracies. It is from the British that we have inherited the concept that a man is innocent until he is proven guilty.

Today crude and sinister men are trying to destroy this concept, and to shake the very foundations of our freedom based on the due process of law. Witch hunters are on the loose again, often cloaked with immunity, and armed with subpoenas and the cruel whiplash of unevaluated gossip.

History is filled with examples of temporary mob excitement, stirred by false or exaggerated charges, resulting in injury to innocent people. On various occasions, down through the years, mass hysteria has gripped the populace for temporary periods, resulting in a witch hunt.

There is a common pattern in the development of this hysteria.

Usually, it takes root in an atmosphere of war, severe economic crisis, or a threat of either. Insecurity is a fruitful breeding ground for such a movement.

In an atmosphere of this kind demagogues or other unprincipled individuals can more easily stir up emotional and irrational fear.

Charges are hurled indiscriminately to an extent that they are directed at obviously innocent individuals. Frequently some of the precious civil rights for which men have fought for centuries are thrown to the winds in the wild effort to make some of the charges stick.

Ignorance and superstition are the principal tools of demagogues as they attempt to inflame mob excitement.

Racial, religious and class animosities are stirred up to add fuel to the flame. Smear attacks are directed against individuals who are the staunchest advocates of liberal and progressive principles.

I should like to talk today about mass hysteria and witch-hunting in American history, and the causes and symptoms of the major outbreaks. I hope I may be able to furnish some clues to help identify such movements in our time.

I hope this nation will always stand as a citadel of freedom of thought and freedom of speech.

In the world of today, this will not be easy.

We have witnessed the most violent and the most relentless attacks on freedom of the mind that have ever been launched in all history. A few years ago, the Nazis tried to destroy the intellectual and moral achievements of centuries under a wave of hate and prejudice. Today the great foe of the free mind is communism.

Soviet Communism binds the mind of man with the chains of the police state, controlling thought and punishing any deviation with new refinements of brutality.

Communism has never amounted to much as a political movement in this country. Its great threat comes from its support by a foreign government that seeks to maintain a fifth column in the United States. We should be constantly on the alert and vigilant, to resist its efforts to infiltrate our society.

In making this fight, we should be sure that we do not fall into the trap of adopting the totalitarian tactics of the communists themselves.

The nature of the communist conspiracy is such that in combating it we have had to scrutinize, very closely, the lives of many citizens. This is part of the struggle against espionage. But in resisting the enemy, we must not tear ourselves apart.

This is what the demagogues among us would have us do. They are playing on our fears to further partisan political ends. They are playing on our fears to such a degree as to create distrust of some of our greatest institutions — our institutions of education and of religion.

Our institutions of learning are one of our strongest defenses against communism because they are dedicated to the truth. So long as we have free discussion and free inquiry in our colleges and universities, we need not fear that they will fall under the spell of communism. Truth is the product of the clash of minds and ideas which is constantly going on in our institutions of learning, and communism cannot withstand the truth.

We have always followed the policy in this country that the government, while it may support education, should never control it. Neither the Congress—nor the Federal government, nor the State governments should put limitations on freedom of thought in our institutions of learning. The standards of a university or a college are standards of intellectual integrity. They can be applied far better by the men responsible for the administration of our institutions of learning than by men in the State legislatures or the Congress, who have not devoted their lives to the special problems of education.

Remember what Jefferson said: "I have sworn upon the altar of God eternal hostility against every form of tyranny over the mind of man."

Our educational institutions, like all our human institutions, are subject to human frailties and human errors. There is no mortal way to assure their absolute perfection. But I submit that our universities are the best judges of the integrity of their own teachers, and it is far safer to let them police themselves than to subject them to political censorship.

The infamous Salem witchcraft "delusion" of Sixteen Hundred and Ninety-two is a striking demonstration of the way in which mob hysteria can deprive the individual of common justice and injure innocent people.

The number of actual executions—twenty—was small in comparison with the mass murder of Jews by the Nazis. Nevertheless, there were some of the same elements of primitive violence involved on a localized scale.

There were many unsettling factors which made the community of Salem more susceptible to hysteria.

Lawlessness, in the form of privateering, was increasing. The new governor of Massachusetts, Sir William Phips, was incompetent. Taxation was unusually burdensome falling mostly on the struggling, small settlers.

People believed in witches and demons. The threat of the devil was a popular theme for use against wavering members of congregations.

Reverend Samuel Parris, the minister of Salem Village, had two slaves in his household from the West Indies. The younger girls of the community, including Reverend Parris' daughter Betty, soon discovered that one of them had a fascinating grasp of the art of fortune-telling. They asked her to teach them this art in secret meetings always in fear of being discovered by their elders. These young girls soon began to exhibit disturbing emotional symptoms, such as weeping, day-dreaming, incoherent speech, and, in more serious cases, convulsions.

Dr. William Griggs was called in to examine the malady and he tried to diagnose it. Unable to discover what was wrong, he finally concluded that these girls were influenced by an evil spirit.

Induced to name their "tormentors" the girls implicated others. Court was set up on a street corner before which many were hauled.

Charges, counter-charges, and widespread name-calling followed as the excitement mounted to a fever pitch.

Many were accused on the basis of "spectral evidence"—the afflicted person claimed that the "shape" of the accused had cast its spell.

Such evidence was difficult to refute. At each denial by the accused in the courtroom, the "afflicted" girls would scream or fall into convulsions, convincing most people present that this was indeed proof of witchcraft.

The plague of hysteria swept through Salem, and no individual seemed entirely safe from accusation. It was impossible to tell where the finger of suspicion would fall next, for some of the most respected citizens of the community were accused and hustled off to prison on the flimsiest evidence.

The overwrought populace even reached up into Maine to drag back and hang Reverend George Burroughs, who ten years before had been Salem's pastor and whose "spectral shape" was accused of witchcraft.

Nineteen persons from Salem, mostly women, were hanged on Gallows Hill and one was "pressed to death" all in response to the demands of the accusers and the vigilance of Reverend Parris in trying to drive out the devil.

In the fall of Sixteen Hundred and Ninety-two, the hysteria started to decline. When the accusations touched more and more people close to the very prosecutors and ministers themselves, the populace was shocked into a realization that the community was slowly committing suicide.

In subsequent years, many of the accusers and prosecutors publicly confessed their error for the part they had played in the witchcraft's hysteria. The names of the victims were publicly cleared. Now only last month in the year of 1954, two hundred and sixty-two years later, the State of Massachusetts has officially declared that those hanged were innocent.

About one hundred years later, in 1798 to 1800, a mass hysteria of greater proportions swept the country and culminated in the Alien and Sedition Laws.

This developed when France which had been our ally in our Revolution seemed to have been transformed from a friend into a threatening enemy.

At the same time, the majority of Americans were rising up politically against the Federalist party. Unscrupulous politicians tried to play on this fear of France in such a way as to injure the growing power of Jeffersonian democracy.

These events unfolded only a few years after the French Revolution. The ideals of "Liberty, Equality and Fraternity" enunciated during the French Revolution appealed to the democratic-minded Jeffersonians, while the aristocratic-minded Federalists looked on the French Revolution as an example of mob madness.

Riding on the crest of a wave of anti-French feeling in 1798, the Federalists decided to take additional steps to crush the Jeffersonian opposition in advance of the mid-term congressional elections.

French and Irish immigrants had a habit of lining up over-whelmingly against the Federalists in elections, so steps were taken to curb alien influence.

Additional measures were taken to choke off other domestic political opposition to the Federalists.

As a result the Alien and Sedition Laws were passed, vesting in the government very drastic arbitrary powers. There were four statutes: the Naturalization Act, the Alien Act, the Enemy Alien Act, and the Sedition Act.

The most drastic of the four statutes was the Sedition Act.

The Sedition Act was directed against persons who uttered or published "false, scandalous, and malicious writings against the government of the United States, or either House of the Congress . . . or the President, with intent to defame."

The penalty was a fine of up to Two Thousand Dollars and imprisonment up to two years.

The prosecutions made under the Sedition Act were against Jeffersonian Republican newspapers and prominent Jeffersonian political leaders.

It was more than coincidence that all the prosecutions were against those who were unfriendly toward President Adams and the Federalist Party, and there was no attempt to proceed against any newspaper or individual who criticized Vice-President Jefferson with an equal or greater degree of abuse.

In the early spring of Eighteen Hundred, a petition for the repeal of the Sedition Law was prepared and circulated. It was a powerful and vituperative petition. In Otsego County, New York, signatures for the petition were solicited by Jedekiah Peck, a kindly, eccentric itinerant, whose main occupation was preaching the gospel and surveying.

But even Peck could not escape the wrath of the Federalists, and the Sedition Act itself was invoked against him. A grand jury was empaneled in New York and a bench warrant sworn out for his arrest. Dragged from his bed at midnight, and manacled like a dangerous criminal, Peck was started on the two hundred mile journey down to New York.

The case backfired for the Federalists, however, for the roads were bad and the journey so slow that the news of his arrest spread ahead of him, and sympathetic crowds cheered him at many villages along the way. By illustrating the Federalist conception of Liberty, Peck actually turned popular opinion against the repressive measures of the Federalists.

As with the Salem witchcraft prosecutions, those sentenced under the Sedition Act (or in most cases their survivors) received monetary restitution in later years.

The ill-fated attempt of the Federalists to snuff out opposition by crushing the liberty of the people resulted in an overwhelming defeat for the Federalists in the election of Eighteen Hundred. Never again did the Federalists regain power. Unfortunately, however, the type of hysteria and witch-hunting which the Federalists sponsored did not die with the election of Eighteen Hundred.

The next wave of hysteria was the anti-masonic movement directed against the Masonic Order, on the grounds that there were evils inherent in the secrecy and rituals of masonry. As with other witch-hunts, it is difficult to reduce the rationale of the movement to cold logic; it was a form of anti-religious hysteria, similar in nature to the many anti-Catholic movements in the years which followed.

Peculiarly enough, anti-masonry was launched during a period of liberalism in politics, when Jacksonian Democracy was in full bloom. More and more classes of people were being extended the right to vote, the rights of labor were being gradually recognized, and social and humanitarian reforms were receiving support. These stirrings of liberalism bred reactions from propertied interests, scared by the spread of economic and political democracy. The political strength of the anti-masonic movement was absorbed and cultivated by the opponents of Andrew Jackson, who tried in vain to ride to political victory on the hysteria and prejudice of this intolerant movement.

Political leaders in rural areas in the north—particularly in New York and Pennsylvania—whipped up the emotional fervor of anti-masonry in an attempt to get enough votes to offset the Jacksonian Democrats. Behind the scenes, financial encouragement to the anti-masons was given by those who felt that Andrew Jackson and his party represented a threat to the interests of the wealthy.

The anti-masonic movement was touched off in Eighteen Hundred and Twenty-six by the disappearance of a bricklayer named William Morgan, a Mason of Batavia, New York, who had fallen into disrepute with his lodge. Morgan had threatened to publish a book revealing the innermost secrets of the Masonic Order, and his sudden disappearance raised suspicion that the Masons had murdered him in order to protect their secrets. The incident touched off a wave of anti-masonic hysteria. In the press, from the pulpit, and on the political hustings, emotional attacks on the Masons were delivered.

More serious and damaging, of course, was the spirit of intolerance and persecution engendered by the Anti-Masonic Movement. Politicians stirred up the hysteria in an effort to get votes, using anti-masonry as an issue because they had no genuine issues.

By Eighteen Hundred and Forty, organized anti-masonry was dead. The hate and intolerance which it had engendered, however, were not. They were merely channeled in another direction, and the fanatics soon found a new cause of intolerance in the Know-Nothing Movement.

The so-called Know-Nothing Movement was primarily directed against Catholics and immigrants in the period prior to the Civil War. It was a native American phenomenon, characterized by a super-nationalistic feeling, hatred of certain minority groups, and secrecy of code and operation.

The name derived from the fact that members who were questioned about the organization usually replied, "I Know Nothing." In later years, the political supporters of the movement succeeded in getting on the ballot in many states as the "American Party."

Although the American Indian is probably the only native American, some individuals have always imagined that immigration is a menace to American institutions.

The immigrants settled in huge numbers in large urban areas, where many of them joined city political machines. The Know-Nothing Movement started as a protest against the influence of these immigrants. It was directed against the Germans in Cincinnati and St. Louis, the Scandinavians in Wisconsin and Minnesota, and the Irish in the east. Primarily, however, it was directed against the Catholics. All who joined were pledged to vote only for natives, to press for the enactment of a twenty-one year probationary period preceding naturalization, and to combat the Catholic Church.

The prejudice against the Catholics was stirred up by books and pamphlets, speeches and sermons, and the same pattern developed as in the Anti-Masonic Movement. The background was laid by declarations that the Pope was scheming to set up a Catholic State in America.

Mob hysteria broke out into overt attacks on Catholics, such as the burning and pillaging of the Ursuline Convent at Charlestown, Massachusetts; riots in Boston; the tarring and feathering of Catholic priests; the wrecking of a Catholic church in Manchester, New Hampshire; and riots against Catholic workers on the Baltimore and Ohio Railroad and on the Chesapeake and Ohio Canal. All of these mob actions were a prelude to the more widely organized political activities of the anti-Catholics.

Despite the eventual political decline of the Know-Nothing Movement, the spirit of intolerance was not competely erased. Know-Nothingism fore-shadowed later political and social movements which displayed the same unfortunate religious or racial bigotry, hysteria and witch-hunting.

The spirit of Know-Nothingism came to life again after World War One. Fear of foreigners and fear of organized labor were manipulated and brought together in the radical scare of the twenties, and in the revival of the Ku Klux Klan. Here again fear was stirred up for political purposes. Educational institutions were attacked. The Catholic religion and the Jewish religion were slandered and vilified. As a result, in many States the Ku Klux Klan rose to considerable political importance.

The Klan, like those other hate movements, was ultimately wiped out by the common sense of the American people.

These are some of the periods in our history when witch-hunts and hysteria violated fundamental liberties which mankind has struggled for centuries to secure.

At times the government itself has fallen victim to this hysteria and has taken repressive measures which have interfered with time-honored rights like freedom of the press and freedom of speech.

At other times, dominant groups in various communities have encouraged bigotry and ridden roughshod over the rights of minority groups.

Fortunately, these periods of hysteria have been temporary in nature, and in the long run reason has prevailed.

The American system has been able to survive because its strength is in the Bill of Rights.

Not only does the Bill of Rights protect against Federal infringement of freedom of worship, freedom of speech, freedom of the press and other basic rights, but it shines as a beacon of inspiration in the struggle to preserve civil liberties.

To preserve these liberties, we must have courage and alertness. "Eternal vigilance is" still "the price of liberty."

George Washington warned this nation to guard against the "impostures of pretended patriotism."

Once again we are witnessing the return of the political bogeymen who proclaim themselves custodians of our freedom. They are making a mockery of the very institutions they so callously pretend they are seeking to preserve.

They have no more respect for the due process of law and order than the communists they say they hate but whose methods they copy. These descendants of the ancient order of witch-hunters have learned nothing from history. They care nothing for history. They care less for the American traditions of law and order and fair play.

There is even one among them whose torrent of wild charges is calculated to damage the faith of Americans in the integrity of their government, army, schools, churches, their labor unions, and the press. Most of all he is threatening to undermine the respect and confidence Americans must have in one another.

The cause of freedom both at home and abroad is damaged when a great country yields to hysteria.

The way for us to spread democracy is to practice it ourselves.

In times such as these, our colleges and universities have a very special obligation to maintain freedom of thought and inquiry.

The precious freedoms for which Westminster College stands— freedom of thought and freedom of the human spirit—are our greatest strength in the world struggle in which we are involved. We cannot win our goals by abandoning our values. I urge you to be alert and bold in preserving and protecting our democratic freedoms.

CHAPTER IX

Veto of the Immigration and Nationality Act of 1952

A message to the House of Representatives of the Congress of the United States from President Harry S. Truman, June 25, 1952. (From the *Congressional Record*, Eighty-second Congress, Second session. LXXXXVIII, pt. 6, pp. 8082-8085.)

To the House of Representatives:

I return herewith, without my approval, H. R. 5678, the proposed Immigration and Nationality Act.

In outlining my objections to this bill, I want to make it clear that it contains certain provisions that meet with my approval. This is a long and complex piece of legislation. It has 164 separate sections, some with more than 40 sub-divisions. It presents a difficult problem of weighing the good against the bad, and arriving at a judgment ·on the whole.

H. R. 5678 is an omnibus bill which would revise and codify all of our laws relating to immigration, naturalization, and nationality.

A general revision and modernization of these laws unquestionably is needed and long overdue, particularly with respect to immigration. But this bill would not provide us with an immigration policy adequate for the present world situation. Indeed, the bill, taking all its provisions together, would be a step backward and not a step forward. In view of the crying need for reform in the field of immigration, I deeply regret that I am unable to approve H. R. 5678.

In recent years, our immigration policy has become a matter of major national concern. Long dormant questions about the effect of our immigration laws now assume first-rate importance. What we do in the field of immigration and naturalization is vital to the continued growth and internal development of the United States—to the economic and social strength of our country—which is the core of the defense of the free world. Our immigration policy is equally, if not more, important to the conduct of our foreign relations and to our responsibilities of moral leadership in the struggle for world peace.

In one respect, this bill recognizes the great international significance of our immigration and naturalization policy, and takes a step to improve existing laws. All racial bars to naturalization would be removed, and at least some minimum immigration quota would be afforded to each of the free nations of Asia.

I have long urged that racial or national barriers to naturalization be abolished. This was one of the recommendations in my civil rights message to the Congress on February 2, 1948. On February 19, 1951, the House of Representatives unanimously passed a bill to carry it out.

But now this most desirable provision comes before me embedded in a mass of legislation which would perpetuate injustices of long standing against many other nations of the world, hamper the efforts we are making to rally the men of east and west alike to the cause of freedom, and intensify the repressive and inhumane aspects of our immigration procedures. The price is too high, and in good conscience I cannot agree to pay it.

I want all our residents of Japanese ancestry, and all our friends throughout the Far East, to understand this point clearly. I cannot take the step I would like to take and strike down the bars that prejudice has erected against them, without, at the same time, establishing new discriminations against the people of Asia and approving harsh and repressive measures directed at all who seek a new life within our boundaries. I am sure that with a little more time and a little more discussion in this country the public conscience and the good sense of the American people will assert themselves, and we shall be in a position to enact an immigration and naturalization policy that will be fair to all.

In addition to removing racial bars to naturalization, the bill would permit American women citizens to bring their alien husbands to this country as non-quota immigrants, and enable alien husbands of resident women aliens to come in under the quota in a preferred status. These provisions would be a step toward preserving the integrity of the family under our immigration laws, and are clearly desirable.

The bill would also relieve transportation companies of some of the unjustified burdens and penalties now imposed upon them. In particular, it would put an end to the archaic requirement that carriers pay the expenses of aliens detained at the port of entry, even though such aliens have arrived with proper travel documents.

But these few improvements are heavily outweighed by other provisions of the bill which retain existing defects in our laws, and add many undesirable new features.

The bill would continue, practically without change, the national origins quota system, which was enacted into law in 1924, and put into effect in 1929. This quota system—always based upon assumptions at variance with our American ideals—is long since out of date and more than ever unrealistic in the face of present world conditions.

This system hinders us in dealing with current immigration problems, and is a constant handicap in the conduct of our foreign relations. As I stated in my message to Congress on March 24, 1952, on the need for an emergency program of immigration from Europe:

> Our present quota system is not only inadequate to meet present emergency needs, it is also an obstacle to the development of an enlightened and satisfactory immigration policy for the long-run future.

The inadequacy of the present quota system has been demonstrated since the end of the war, when we were compelled to resort to emergency legislation to admit displaced persons. If the quota system remains unchanged, we shall be compelled to resort to similar emergency legislation again, in order to admit any substantial portion of the refugees from communism or the victims of overcrowding in Europe.

With the idea of quotas in general there is no quarrel. Some numerical limitation must be set, so that immigration will be within our capacity to absorb. But the over-all limitation of numbers imposed by the national origins quota system is too small for our needs today, and the country by country limitations create a pattern that is insulting to large numbers of our finest citizens, irritating to our allies abroad, and foreign to our purposes and ideals.

The over-all quota limitation, under the law of 1924, restricted annual immigration to approximately 150,000. This was about one-seventh of 1 per cent of our total population in 1920. Taking into account the growth in population since 1920, the law now allows us but one-tenth of 1 per cent of our total population. And since the largest national quotas are only partly used, the number actually coming in has been in the neighborhood of one-fifteenth of 1 per cent. This is far less than we must have in the years ahead to keep up with the growing needs of our Nation for man-power to maintain the strength and vigor of our economy.

The greatest vice of the present quota system, however, is that it discriminates, deliberately and intentionally, against many of the peoples of the world. The purpose behind it was to cut down and virtually eliminate immigration to this country from southern and eastern Europe. A theory was invented to rationalize this objective. The theory was that in order to be readily assimilable, European immigrants should be admitted in proportion to the numbers of persons of their respective national stocks already here as shown by the census of 1920. Since Americans of English, Irish, and German descent were most numerous, immigrants of those three nationalities got the lion's share—more than two-thirds—of the total quota. The remaining third was divided up among all the other nations given quotas.

The desired effect was obtained. Immigration from the newer sources of southern and eastern Europe was reduced to a trickle. The quotas allotted to England and Ireland remained largely unused, as was intended. Total quota immigration fell to a half or third—and sometimes even less—of the annual limit of 154,000. People from such countries as Greece or Spain or Latvia were virtually deprived of any opportunity to come here at all, simply because Greeks or Spaniards or Latvians had not come here before 1920 in any substantial numbers.

The idea behind this discriminatory policy was, to put it baldly, that Americans with English or Irish names were better people and better citizens than Americans with Italian or Greek or Polish names. It was thought that people of west European origin made better citizens than Rumanians or Yugoslavs or Ukrainians or Hungarians or Balts or Austrians. Such a concept is utterly unworthy of our traditions and our ideals. It violates the great political doctrine of the Declaration of Independence that "all men are created equal." It denies the humanitarian creed inscribed beneath the Statue of Liberty proclaiming to all nations, "Give me your tired, your poor, your huddled masses yearning to breathe free."

It repudiates our basic religious concepts, our belief in the brotherhood of man, and in the words of St. Paul, "there is neither Jew or Greek, there is neither bond nor free, for ye are all one in Christ Jesus."

The basis of this quota system was false and unworthy in 1924. It is even worse now. At the present time, this quota system keeps out the very people we want to bring in. It is incredible to me that, in this year of 1952, we should again be enacting into law such a slur on the patriotism, the capacity, and the decency of a large part of our citizenry.

Today, we have entered into an alliance, the North Atlantic Treaty, with Italy, Greece, and Turkey against one of the most terrible threats mankind has ever faced. We are asking them to join with us in protecting the peace of the world. We are helping them to build their defences, and train their men, in the common cause. But through this bill, we say to their people: You are less worthy to come to this country than Englishmen or Irishmen; you Italians, who need to find homes abroad in the hundreds of thousands—you shall have a quota of 5,645; you Greeks, struggling to assist the helpless victims of a Communist civil war—you shall have a quota of 308; and you Turks, you are brave defenders of the eastern flank, but you shall have a quota of only 225.

Today we are protecting ourselves, as we were in 1924, against being flooded by immigrants from Eastern Europe. This is fantastic. The countries of Eastern Europe have fallen under the Communist yoke; they are silenced, fenced off by barbed wire and mine fields; no one passes their borders but at the risk of his life. We do not need to be protected against immigrants from these countries; on the contrary, we want to stretch out a helping hand, to save those who have managed to flee into Western Europe, to succor those who are brave enough to escape from barbarism, to welcome and restore them against the day when their countries will, as we hope, be free again. But this we cannot do, as we would like to do, because the quota for Poland is only 6,500, as against the 138,000 exiled Poles all over Europe, who are asking to come to these shores; because the quota for the now subjugated Baltic countries is little more than 700, against the 23,000 Baltic refugees imploring us to admit them to a new life here; because the quota for Rumania is only 289, and some 30,000 Rumanians who have managed to escape the labor camps and the mass deportations of their Soviet masters, have asked our help. These are only a few examples of the absurdity, the cruelty of carrying over into this year of 1952 the isolationist limitations of our 1924 law.

In no other realms of our national life are we so hampered and stultified by the dead hand of the past as we are in the field of immigration. We do not limit our cities to their 1920 boundaries; we do not hold corporations to their 1920 capitalizations; we welcome progress and change to meet changing condition in every sphere of life except in the field of immigration.

The time to shake off this dead weight of past mistakes is now. The time to develop a decent policy of immigration—a fitting instrument for our foreign policy and a true reflection of the ideals we stand for, at home and abroad—is now. In my earlier message on immigration, I tried to explain to the Congress that the situation we face in immigration is an emergency—that it must be met promptly. I have pointed out that in the last few years we have blazed a new trail in immigration, through our displaced persons program. Through the combined efforts of the Government and private agencies, working together not to keep people out, but to bring qualified people in, we summoned our resources of good will and human feeling to meet the task. In this program, we have found better techniques to meet the immigration problems of the 1950's.

None of this fruitful experience of the last 3 years is reflected in this bill before me. None of the crying human needs of this time of trouble is recognized in this bill. But it is not too late. The Congress can remedy these defects, and it can adopt legislation to meet the most critical problems before adjournment.

The only consequential change in the 1924 quota system which the bill would make is to extend a small quota to each of the countries of Asia. But most of the beneficial effects of this gesture are offset by other provisions of the bill. The countries of Asia are told in one breath that they shall have quotas for their nationals, and in the next, that the nationals of the other countries, if their ancestry is as much as 50 per cent Asian, shall be charged to these quotas.

It is only with respect to persons of oriental ancestry that this invidious discrimination applies. All other persons are charged to the country of their birth. But persons with Asian ancestry are charged to the countries of Asia, wherever they may have been born, or however long their ancestors have made their homes outside the land of their origin. These provisions are without justification.

I now wish to turn to the other provisions of the bill, those dealing with the qualifications of aliens and immigrants for admission, with the administration of the laws, and with problems of naturalization and nationality. In these provisions, too, I find objections that preclude my signing this bill.

The bill would make it even more difficult to enter our country. Our resident aliens would be more easily separated from homes and families under grounds of deportation, both new and old, which would specifically be made retroactive. Admission to our citizenship would be made more difficult; expulsion from our citizenship would be made easier. Certain rights of native born, first generation Americans would be limited. All our citizens returning from abroad would be subjected to serious risk of unreasonable invasions of privacy. Seldom has a bill exhibited the distrust evidenced here for citizens and aliens alike— at a time when we need unity at home, and the confidence of our friends abroad.

We have adequate and fair provisions in our present law to protect us against the entry of criminals. The changes made by the bill in those provisions would result in empowering minor immigration and consular officials to act as prosecutor, judge, and jury in determining whether acts constituting a crime have been committed. Worse, we would be compelled to exclude certain people because they have been convicted by "courts" in Communist countries that know no justice. Under this provision, no matter how construed, it would not be possible for us to admit many of the men and women who have stood up against totalitarian repression and have been punished for doing so. I do not approve of substituting totalitarian vengeance for democratic justice. I will not extend full faith and credit to the judgments of the Communist secret police.

The realities of a world only partly free would again be ignored in the provision flatly barring entry to those who made misrepresentations in securing visas. To save their lives and the lives of loved ones still imprisoned, refugees from tyranny sometimes misstate various details of their lives. We do not want to encourage fraud. But we must recognize that conditions in some parts of the world drive our friends to desperate steps. An exception restricted to cases involving misstatement of country of birth is not sufficient. And to make refugees from oppression forever deportable on such technical grounds is shabby treatment, indeed.

Some of the new grounds of deportation which the bill would provide are unnecessarily severe. Defects and mistakes in admission would serve to deport at any time because of the bill's elimination, retroactively as well as prospectively, of the present humane provision barring deportations on such grounds 5 years after entry. Narcotic drug addicts would be deportable at any time, whether or not the addiction was culpable, and whether or not cured. The threat of deportation would drive the addict into hiding beyond the reach of cure, and the danger to the country from drug addiction would be increased.

I am asked to approve the reenactment of highly objectionable provisions now contained in the Internal Security Act of 1950—a measure passed over my veto shortly after the invasion of South Korea. Some of these provisions would empower the Attorney General to deport any alien who has engaged or has had a purpose to engage in activities "prejudicial to the public interest" or "subversive to the national security." No standards or definitions are provided to guide discretion in the exercise of powers so sweeping. To punish undefined "activities" departs from traditional American insistence on established standards of guilt. To punish an undefined "purpose" is thought control.

These provisions are worse than the infamous Alien Act of 1798, passed in a time of national fear and distrust of foreigners, which gave the President power to deport any alien deemed "dangerous to the peace and safety of the United States." Alien residents were thoroughly frightened and citizens much disturbed by that threat to liberty.

Such powers are inconsistent with our democratic ideals. Conferring powers like that upon the Attorney General is unfair to him as well as to our alien residents. Once fully informed of such vast discretionary powers vested in the Attorney General, Americans now would and should be just as alarmed as Americans were in 1798 over less drastic powers vested in the President.

Heretofore, for the most part, deportation and exclusion have rested upon findings of fact made upon evidence. Under this bill, they would rest in many instances upon the "opinion" or "satisfaction" of immigration or consular employees. The change from objective findings to subjective feelings is not compatible with our system of justice. The result would be to restrict or eliminate judicial review of unlawful administrative action.

The bill would sharply restrict the present opportunity of citizens and alien residents to save family members from deportation. Under the procedures of present law, the Attorney General can exercise his discretion to suspend deportation in meritorious cases. In each such case, at the present time, the exercise of administrative discretion is subject to the scrutiny and approval of the Congress. Nevertheless, the bill would prevent this discretion from being used in many cases where it is now available, and would narrow the circle of those who can obtain relief from the letter of the law. This is most unfortunate, because the bill, in its other provisions, would impose harsher restrictions and greatly increase the number of cases deserving equitable relief.

Native-born American citizens who are dual nationals would be subjected to loss of citizenship on grounds not applicable to other native-born American citizens. This distinction is a slap at millions of Americans whose fathers were of alien birth.

Children would be subjected to additional risk of loss of citizenship. Naturalized citizens would be subjected to the risk of denaturalization by any procedure that can be found to be permitted under any State law or practice pertaining to minor civil lawsuits. Judicial review of administrative denials of citizenship would be severely limited and impeded in many cases and completely eliminated in others. I believe these provisions raise serious constitutional questions. Constitutionality aside, I see no justification in national policy for their adoption.

Section 401 of this bill would establish a Joint Congressional Committee on Immigration and Nationality Policy. This committee would have the customary powers to hold hearings and to subpoena witnesses, books, papers, and documents. But the committee would also be given powers over the executive branch which are unusual and of a highly questionable nature. Specifically, section 401 would provide that "the Secretary of State and the Attorney General shall without delay submit to the committee all regulations, instructions, and all other information as requested by the committee relative to the administration of this act."

This section appears to be another attempt to require the executive branch to make available to the Congress administrative documents, .communications between the President and his subordinates, confidential files, and other records of that character. It also seems to imply that the committee would undertake to supervise or approve regulations. Such proposals are not consistent with the constitutional doctrine of the separation of powers.

In these and many other respects, the bill raises basic questions as to our fundamental immigration and naturalization policy, and the laws and practices for putting that policy into effect.

Many of the aspects of the bill which have been most widely criticized in the public debate are reaffirmations or elaboration of existing statutes or administrative procedures. Time and again, examination discloses that the revisions of existing law that would be made by the bill are intended to solidify some restrictive practice of our immigration authorities, or to overrule or modify some ameliorative decision of the Supreme Court or other Federal courts. By and large, the changes that would be made by the bill do not depart from the basically restrictive spirit of our existing laws—but intensify and reinforce it.

These conclusions point to an underlying condition which deserves the most careful study. Should we not undertake a reassessment of our immigration policies and practices in the light of the conditions that face us in the second half of the twentieth century? The great popular interest which this bill has created, and the criticism which it has stirred up, demand an affirmative answer. I hope the Congress will agree to a careful reexamination of this entire matter.

To assist in this complex task, I suggest the creation of a representative commission of outstanding Americans to examine the basic assumptions of our immigration policy, the quota system and all that goes with it, the effect of our present immigration and nationality laws, their administration, and the ways in which they can be brought into line with our national ideals and our foreign policy.

Such a commission should, I believe, be established by the Congress. Its membership should be bipartisan and divided equally among persons from private life and persons from public life. I suggest that four members be appointed by the President, four by the President of the Senate, and four by the Speaker of the House of Representatives. The commission should be given sufficient funds to employ a staff and it should have adequate powers to hold hearings, take testimony, and obtain information. It should make a report to the President and to the Congress within a year from the time of its creation.

Pending the completion of studies by such a commission, and the consideration of its recommendations by the Congress, there are certain steps which I believe it is most important for the Congress to take this year.

First, I urge the Congress to enact legislation removing racial barriers against Asians from our laws. Failure to take this step profits us nothing and can only have serious consequences for our relations with the peoples of the Far East. A major contribution to this end would be the prompt enactment by the Senate of H. R. 403. That bill, already passed by the House of Representatives, would remove the racial bars to the naturalization of Asians.

Second, I strongly urge the Congress to enact the temporary, emergency immigration legislation which I recommended 3 months ago. In my message of March 24, 1952, I advised the Congress that one of the gravest problems arising from the present world crisis is created by the overpopulation in parts of Western Europe. That condition is aggravated by the flight and explusion of people from behind the iron curtain. In view of these serious problems, I asked the Congress to authorize the admission of 300,000 additional immigrants to the United States over a 3-year period. These immigrants would include Greek nationals, Dutch nationals, Italians from Italy and Trieste, Germans and persons of German ethnic origin, and religious and political refugees from communism in Eastern Europe. This temporary program is urgently needed. It is very important that the Congress act upon it this year. I urge the Congress to give prompt and favorable consideration to the bills introduced by Senator Hendrickson and Representative Celler (S. 3109 and H. R. 7376), which will implement the recommendations contained in my message of March 24.

I very much hope that the Congress will take early action on these recommendations. Legislation to carry them out will correct some of the unjust provisions of our laws, will strengthen us at home and abroad, and will serve to relieve a great deal of the suffering and tension existing in the world today.

6.00